This book is fantastic!!! Very solid strategies.... ... ... when I first got out of school!! Most health professionals, including myself, haven't had any business classes, so it's a guessing game as to where to turn! This definitely shortens the learning curve dramatically!! It's a MUST HAVE for anyone who wants to be a successful entrepreneur!

Christopher R. Mohr, PhD, RD, CSSD
Owner, Mohr Results, Inc., www.MohrResults.com

Margie is a genius as she skillfully guides business owners to overcome one of the toughest challenges—time management. Margie arms readers with a plan to efficiently make the most of their time by providing practical and useful strategies to prioritize and get organized. Margie's book will give you direction and a sense of "I can do this!" Her advice and support is priceless!

Lyssie Lakatos, RD, CDN and Tammy Lakatos Shames, RD, CDN
The Nutrition Twins®, www.nutritiontwins.com

Just Jump explores two essentials of any new business: the business plan and the marketing plan. Sound scary? Marjorie makes it manageable so you won't get stuck in the terminology—and instead begin to visualize its success.

Joanne Lichten, PhD, RD does business as "Dr. Jo" writing books,
doing spokesperson work, and speaking at conferences about
How to Make More Dough., www.drjo.com.

I wish that I'd had Margie's book 15 years ago when I started my own private practice. Her guide is practical, refreshingly concise, and motivating. Margie gives us the tools to turn our dream into reality. Don't delay—get your hands on *Just Jump* and start growing the business of your dreams.

Ellen Coleman, MA, MPH, RD, CSSD
Author, *Diet, Exercise, and Fitness,* 7th ed., *Nutrition Dimension*

With careful thought and consideration the 72 exercises in this book are sure to prepare you to start a successful business.

Linda S. Eck Mills, MBA, RD, LDN, FADA Professional Speaker /
Educator Dynamic Communication Services, 610-488-7010
www.theconsultantsforum.com/eckmills.

So many health and fitness professionals fantasize about quitting the daily grind and opening up their own businesses. This book helps you make that fantasy a reality by providing you with the tools you need to make it happen. If you lack the business confidence to go for your dream, then this is a must

continued

read. The thought provoking exercises will help you define your direction as you build a workable business plan. If you follow the steps outlined in this book, you will soon be on the road to a more purpose-driven, meaningful career!

Nancy Collins, PhD, RD, LD/N
Nutrition and Health Consultant, www.RD411.com, Weston, FL

Readers will perform valuable exercises that provide insight into just "who is" their ideal client—and how to identify what those clients expect. I especially like one simple exercise in Chapter 6. Geiser suggests you start to identify your niche market in this way: Imagine all your past clients walking into your office. Examine their demographic, psychographic and other attributes. What's important to them? By identifying your ideal client, you'll more easily determine your individual business identity.

Christine M. Palumbo, MBA, RD
Nutrition Communications Consultant, Naperville, Illinois
www.ChristinePalumbo.com

Finally! A book written in plain English by someone who has successfully made the jump to self employment and is willing to share her insights with the rest of us! This book is a must read for anyone in the health and fitness industry who ever considered being their own boss. Marjorie Geiser writes with passion and anticipates your questions in a way that makes you feel she's sitting just across the kitchen table with you, as your own personal coach.

Joe Cannon, MS, CSCS, NSCA-CPT
Author, speaker and self-employed personal trainer, www.Joe-Cannon.com

This book is the perfect fit for anyone wanting to start their own business. It offers a step by step, practical blueprint to create a successful business and avoid the common pitfalls business owners often have. I highly suggest having a copy of this book to be your guide before jumping into your own business.

Meri Raffetto RD, LDN
founder Real Living Nutrition Services, www.reallivingnutrition.com

Margie, this is JUST what I was looking for! Thank you and FANTASTIC job!!! ...this book is a MUST HAVE for fitness professionals who want to start their own business. I remember going to Borders and skimming the shelves but none of the business books really "spoke" to me. I do not consider myself a business savvy person so I needed something that was specific to the fitness industry. *Just Jump* is the roadmap that I have been looking for!

Christina Todd, ACSM-CPT, NSCA-CPT
Fitness Thinktank, The Roving Gym,
www.fitnessthinktank.com, www.therovinggym.com

Just Jump:

The No-Fear Business Start-up Guide for Health and Fitness Professionals

Marjorie Geiser, RD, NSCA-CPT

California Based Publishing
Running Springs, CA

ISBN: 978-0-9814860-0-0
Library of Congress Control Number: 2008902415

Cover and text design by Bookwrights
Printed in the United States of America

California Based Publishing
P.O. Box 1207
Running Springs, CA 92382

Contents

Appendices

Acknowledgments

This book is an excellent example of a process and how nothing ever happens without the help and guidance of others. There are more people I would like to thank, but that would become a book of its own! So, here are the people who most made a difference in the development and creation of "Just Jump":

Thank you to Bea Fields of Bea Fields Companies, Inc at www.beafields.com. I still remember her asking me, "Why not coach other dietitians who want to start a business?" I had never dawned on me before that question! Thank you, Bea!

Next in the process came Ursula Mentjes of Potential Quest, Inc at www.potentialquest.com. When discussing processes with Ursula, she suggested I put my process down on paper. Then she said, "Why not turn it into a book?" Again, hm; that hadn't dawned on me, before! What a great idea, Ursula!

Once I made the decision to start writing a book, I realized I knew NOTHING about this process at all, so I ended up buying a book entitled, "The Well-Fed Self-Publisher" by Peter Bowerman (www.wellfedsp.com). Through Peter's supportive mentoring, I climbed the next hurtles of just figuring out how to get started and how really make it all happen. Peter, your guidance was invaluable.

The next step was editing, to which I am forever grateful to Alisa Griffis from Write Well, Write Now, USA, Inc at www.writewellwritenowusa.com. Alisa spent great amounts of time helping me refine my target audience and change my wording to reach my audience. Thanks for making me 'focus'!

How a book looks, inside and out, can make or break sales, so for that I am forever grateful to Mayapriya Long of Bookwrights at www.bookwrights.com. Not only did Maypriya design something to be proud of, but she also provided invaluable coaching with her excellent design services.

Throughout this process, I have to be sure to thank my VA, Donna Toothaker of 1stVa (www.1stva.com) for all of her great editing support, professional support and basically for being my second right arm. Without the dedicated professionalism of Donna, I couldn't do all that I do, today.

Finally, I never would be this far if it wasn't for the support of my family. To my husband, Don, thanks for your never-ending, even if challenging, support. You have always challenged me to think bigger and in different ways than my own mind might be heading. You never doubted that I could write and publish a book. How much more grateful can you be for that kind of support?

To my mother and daughter who may not have understood what I was doing, but supportive, none-the-less. I make my mother proud and I hope to stand as an example of what's possible for my daughter.

Finally, to all my friends, clients and colleagues who have supported me through the years, thank you! Again, none of us gets to where we are alone, and for that, I am forever grateful. May you all strive for what you believe is possible in your life!

Marjorie Geiser
February, 2008

Introduction

"You only live once – but if you work it right, once is enough."

– Joe E. Lewis

People often dream of the way they'd ideally like things to be in their life. Sometimes they keep those big dreams hidden inside of themselves, not sharing, or sharing with just a few, choice, private people. This may have happened to you, too. Because you've got people close to you, they often will encourage you to "just do it." But we don't always dive in. You know they just love and care about you and want for you whatever you want. But sometimes you're not really sure about that, either, and you're not sure they think you can do it. You look at all the reasons why you shouldn't embark upon a new business adventure, too. You listen to those voices of limitations, doubts. You hear your professors from school, who say, "Get a job as a clinical dietitian," or a boss at that WIC job who says, "Don't be silly; you have a good job, here!" You listen to the other trainers in the club who say, "Yeah, sounds great, but how will you really do it?" Why should YOU be able to accomplish great things? Why should YOU be able to live your dreams, your BIG dreams? And so you stay safe and continue your quiet lives, wondering what it would be like *if* . . . .

I help clients move from that place of staying "safe" into stepping up into their dreams; today they live their vision! I ask them to jump off the cliff, but I teach them how to build wings so they can fly. Just as I do with my weight training clients, I teach clients the basics and help them learn how to listen to themselves. In this book, I will give you the tools to build your confidence, to "Pump you up," so to speak. By the end of the book, you will be strong, confident, and self-assured! You will have the skills that you need to start your own training business and be successful at it. I have practiced all that I share, and today I help those who think it will always just be a dream.

Why *not* live your big dream? Why believe it's just for others? We all have a limited time on this earth. If you don't "go for it," what will you be thinking in 20-40 years from now? It brings tears to my eyes to even CONSIDER looking back at my life regretting not at least *trying* the things I dreamed about! When I hear my own voices of doubt, I will ask myself, "What is the worst that can happen?'"

I'm *not* saying just jump in blindly. You do have to plan, you do have to look at the opportunities, and you do have to determine whether they are realistic and viable. You have to do your due diligence and research – if you want to open your own health club, you need to ask the hard questions such as, what is the likelihood it will succeed; or if you want to open your own office, are there enough physicians who will refer clients to you? And you may have to sweat it out a bit as you dig in deep and spend hours on that research, and grumble that it's not worth it, and you may even believe at times that it's NOT worth it! But, deep in your heart, you will know it is. You want this more than anything. You can feel that desire and passion and excitement, especially knowing you are REALLY GOING FOR IT!

What this book provides

This book is a journey, and I am your travel guide. I will take you from the very conception of what you want, prompting you to look deep within yourself to discover your vision, digging into that place where the passion and drive and desire is to help you create that business of your dreams; your baby (Chapter 1 – Creating your Vision). I will then take you by the hand and encourage you to also look seriously at the fears that have held you back until now, providing you with exercises to help you overcome those fears so you can come out the other end and start forming goals (Chapter 2 – Fears and Limiting Conversations and Chapter 3 - Goals).

From there, you will enter a world of discovery – discovery of who you love to work with (Chapter 5 – Choosing a Niche), what it is about you that draws people to you (Chapter 6 – Your Unique Essence), and how to tell the world what is incredible about you (Chapter 7 – Marketing Message)! You are then primed to put your vision and goals and objectives down on paper, creating those scary "business plans" (Chapter 8 – The Business Plan) and "marketing plans" (Chapter 10 – The Marketing Plan), and finally the marketing calendar (Chapter 11 – The Marketing Calendar), which will take you back to a place of organization you know so well and feel most comfortable with (Chapter 12 – Balance after the Dream is Real).

In order to get the most out of the book, you should do the work and assignments along the way. You can either use a notebook or use the e-book that is available to go with this book. The advantage of the e-book is that you will have forms available to assist you with the work, as well as have access to resources to help you with your research. I suggest filling it out along the way with a pencil because the work you do will be a work in progress and you will find yourself going back and changing things along the way. If you do not have the e-book, however, you can still work through the exercises using a simple notebook.

Who this book is for and what makes it different?

This book is for nutrition and fitness professionals who know their specialty but have allowed fears, doubts, and uncertainty hold them back from seriously taking the steps necessary to build that business of their dreams. There are other books on business for the dietitian, and they are great books that can provide the nuts and bolts of getting a nutrition business up and running. But this book forces you to look into your soul and asks you questions you may have avoided asking yourself. These are real issues that have to be addressed if you ever hope to move out of that investigative stage into the "doing" stage. As an RD, I know how great RDs are at investigating – we can investigate a topic to death! This book is devised to move you into action.

Just as I do with my nutrition clients, I will encourage you to look into the *reasons* for your choices, not just tell you what to do. I will push you to dig in deep within you to answer bigger questions that will instill in you the concept that building a business is building a legacy.

For personal trainers, everything else I have seen to help you start a business reads like "This is how I have done it, so do it this way." Sure, I have done it and can recommended things that work and don't work; however, I am also a student of business and can help you really dig into the aspects of investigation and planning that can ensure your business is on firm ground when you get going. It is not my goal in this book to provide you with another quick way to make a buck; it's a tool to help you build the solid, profitable business of your dreams.

Do I guarantee you will succeed? As a good marketing specialist, I should say, "ABSOLUTELY! Money back guarantee!" As you will read, however, some of the most successful people in business had to fail miserably in order to achieve greatness! Most business owners do suffer some hard times. My own story has **not** all been uphill, either! If you don't have SOME failures, you won't learn as much. But, what I will say, completely from my heart and my complete being, is I know everyone reading this book CAN succeed! It takes passion, drive, determination, refusal to accept defeat, willingness to stick with it, and planning, research, and more planning.

This book is for every person I have heard from or spoken with who has a passion. I have heard it from their heart. Many of you will be reading this book because all you have ever dreamed of since school is to own your own business. Although others may have discouraged you and you have previously allowed those voices to become your own, something continues to draw you to that light of business ownership. Sometimes you just have to jump!

Welcome to the world of entrepreneurship and a new future!

– Margie

First Steps/Discovery:

Ready . . .

CHAPTER 1

Create Your Vision

Desire Is the Fire of Life

If you want something badly enough, you're sure to get it.
If you're willing to pay the price any of your circumstances will change.

Obstacles don't matter very much.
Pain or other circumstances can be there.
But, if you want something bad enough, you'll find a way to get it done.

Reality forms around your commitment to succeed.
Your desires will in time externalize themselves into concrete fact.

You only have to love a thing greatly to get it.
The key to your success is desire.

– Max Stein

You've been dreaming about what it would be like to open your own nutrition or fitness business. It has been on your mind since you were in school, and there are times, especially on Monday mornings, that you daydream about it. Perhaps you're currently a dietitian working in a big hospital, dealing with the drudgery of seeing clients just as they leave the hospital, or having to deal with being treated as "just another body." You may have reduced motivation and you sometimes wonder where the passion went. Or maybe you are a personal trainer working in a health club. You went through all that work to get your degree and now you're also being treated as a "piece of meat," keeping up with quotas and always being pushed to sign up more clients, and in some clubs, push products or eating plans you don't feel comfortable about pushing.

But, you're not really sure what your business will look like. You've got some ideas about how to get started, but maybe you're afraid that you will put your heart and soul into it, only to fail and look like a fool. You barely even talk about it out loud because you don't want family and friends to laugh at you.

Anything can happen if you believe...

Several years ago Jane (not her real name) came to me because she was unhappy with the job where she had been working and felt she needed to determine just what it was she wanted to do as an employee. What she did NOT want to do was work for herself; that was too lofty a consideration! However, through the exercises of discovering her passions, her mission, and her vision, she discovered herself and realized that she could do anything she put her mind to. So, she made a major shift in goals, and today she is a very successful private practitioner working in the corporate wellness industry.

What made a difference for Jane and how can you get to that point? First you must discover yourself, realize how incredible you are, and determine what your vision is for your life and career. You must allow yourself to dream and decide to "go for" that dream.

I am here to tell you that anything is possible! The only limitations you have are the ones you put on yourself! With planning and learning the steps, and doing your homework, if this is something you really want to do, you can do it, AND succeed greatly at it, too! This book walks you through the steps necessary to get you up and running by addressing your fears, determining who you want to be and what you want to create, and helping you create the plans and steps necessary to make your dream a reality.

I'm not saying it's easy! Nothing worth having is. I have had to learn a great deal – about myself, about business, about my clients and potential clients. You will struggle with the questions of what you are all about, what is it about you that will attract potential clients to you and how to spread your marketing message in an exciting way. And it never ends, because your interests and passions will change with the years. But, how exciting the journey is!

Use my story as motivation

When my daughter started kindergarten, I returned to school, too. It took me five years to complete my undergraduate degree in nutrition, but I had a vision: I wanted to help people become healthy and fit in the privacy of their own homes. After school, I didn't have that plan fully in place, even in my mind, but after six years of working in a county hospital as a clinical dietitian, I was ready. I started working on my business plan in 1995 and opened MEG Fitness in June of 1996. MEG Fitness was created to provide in-home personal fitness training to previously unfit adults, mostly peri- and post-menopausal women, with a specialty in post-rehab fitness. I also offered in-home nutrition counseling but provided that as a separate service or as an add-on for training clients.

In 2002, I started looking into coaching as a way to help my clients succeed more effectively. I also wanted to find a way to grow without continuing to run from house to house. My business was a success, but because of my own lack of business know-how, I had failed to plan for how to handle growth! I didn't know how to turn my business into an entity that could survive without me.

As I delved deeper into coaching, I started coaching other nutrition professionals who wanted to start their own private practice. This led me to return to school for an MBA in Entrepreneurship in order to better help my clients not only succeed, but to create that business that *would* survive beyond them. It has been an incredible ride! I'll never look back at my life with regrets that I didn't pursue my dreams. I really have learned that the only limits are those I impose on myself, too! So, I continue to dream bigger and allow my vision to become grander. Why not? What's the worst that can happen??

That's what you have to ask yourself. If you never try, will you be happier? If you never try, how will you know that you could have done it? All successful people in the world have suffered some failures. Taking chances is a big part of entrepreneurship and leadership. Many people think of success and wealth when the name Donald Trump comes to mind, but it's important to remember that he has suffered some great losses in taking chances, too. Athletes such as Michael Jordan have taken as many missed shots as successful ones, but people remember the ones he did make, not the missed ones. Remember that in baseball, members of the Hall of Fame have batting averages around .300. That means that they *failed* to get a base hit 70% of the time! And these are the greatest baseball players in history we're talking about! People who are known for their successes have taken chances and have also suffered some failures. The difference is those failures didn't stop them from trying again; they actually made them stronger by learning from those experiences. They had the knowledge that they could do it and stepped out to prove it!

As you consider what you want to create, you also need to ask yourself if you have the traits of an entrepreneur. An entrepreneur is someone who sees an opportunity and goes for it. It is a person who thinks bigger, beyond just the start-up. It is the person who learns how to best use the resources at hand, such as people, money, and time. It is the person who imagines how what they create will help not only their own bottom line but the community in general as well. And, it is someone who has a tolerance of risk! You have to be willing to risk failure, even at the expense of success.

Right now, you just want to overcome the first hurdle and create a business, but I am going to challenge you to think bigger. It starts with becoming very clear about what your vision is for yourself and for the business you want to create.

My vision is very simple – to empower others to know they can create anything they can imagine. Simple!

The creation of your vision

For the past 33 years, I have looked in the mirror every morning and asked myself, "If today were the last day of my life, would I want to do what I am about to do today?" And whenever the answer has been "No" for too many days in a row, I know I need to change something . . . almost everything – all external expectations, all pride, all fear of embarrassment or failure – these things just fall away in the face of death, leaving only what is truly important. Remembering that you are going to die is the best way I know to avoid the trap of thinking you have something to lose.

– Steve Jobs, CEO of Apple Computer,
Stanford University Commencement Address, 2005

I always ask potential clients this question during our first conversation to help them think of the BIG picture, the big dream: *What would you do if there were no fear of failure?* What is your very first reaction? Do you know? Does your mind go blank? Some people are able to easily tell me, but many are just overwhelmed with the possibility that they COULD do anything and not fail!

I still remember when I was first asked this question. The first thing I thought of was to travel. Notice that it really had NOTHING to do, per se, with my business! The conversation I had after that answer led me to buy my first laptop computer and create the dream I had of working with clients while I traveled the world! I can empower people from anywhere now! I have worked with clients while in Hawaii, on cruise ships, in Rome, in Zurich. Did I mention that anything is possible? What do YOU want to do?

Exercise 1.1

Right now, before you go any farther, answer this question: What would you do if there were no fear of failure? Spend some time thinking about it, if necessary, but don't walk away without writing something. Write it down. Then look at it. Then ask yourself why you are not doing it, and what will it take from you to make it happen?

It is said that one thing that separates leaders from managers is that leaders have a dream *and* the passion to make that dream come true – they don't believe there are limits to what they can achieve. Leaders are the entrepreneurs who begin and grow companies; managers help run those companies. If you are reading this book, chances are you want to become a leader. It's perfectly fine to be happy as a manager, but be okay with it, too!

The challenge for the leader/entrepreneur creating a business is to take that dream and challenge one's self to communicate what that dream is for their organization. What is created is the **vision** of the company.

But how do you discover what your dream is?

It's important to bring up a very critical point here. It is impossible to totally separate your personal vision from your business vision. Your business WILL be you! Your business will be part of who you are and will represent you in all ways. So, if you don't already have a personal vision, start with that first, *then* work on the business vision.

Creating your personal vision will help you gain clarity about what is most important to you, what it is you want, and what you are most passionate about in your life that makes you feel fulfilled. From there you then can create the vision of your ideal business and will have a clearer picture of what that will look like, which will help you clarify your plan and action steps to make it happen.

BZ Riger-Hull, business coach and author of *The Soul of Success* put it this way: "These are the intangible sparks that ignite our drive to move forward and turn the intangible into our reality."

If you already have a business and you are reading this book, did you already make your vision statement? Do you have your personal vision statement? If you answer no, do this exercise also.

Many clients I work with who already own a business lack that vision statement. Heck, *I* didn't have one when I started my business, either! Sure, they may have gone through some of the motions of creating a business plan, but only because they were told they should. Then they packed it away, never to look at again. So this part is for you too.

Put your vision on paper

Now it's time for some more work. Begin by writing down all your thoughts around what your dream is. Never mind that you may think it's just not realistic. This first "idea" session should be free flowing and unedited. It wasn't thought to be realistic to walk on the moon, either! People thought computers were just some fad that would quickly pass, too.

Exercise 1.2

Write your ideas in your e-book or notebook.

Be very specific – don't just say you want to make a lot of money. Close your eyes and envision exactly what you want that business to look like. SEE it and describe it. Again, in the ideal world; this is your dream, so allow yourself to dream big! I will reassure you it won't happen tomorrow, so don't worry (UNLESS you want it to; then, you just have more work to do!). The bigger the dream, the bigger the planning phase will be. And you are in charge, so if you want to grow slowly and achieve that BIG dream in 10 years, that's fine! But come up with that dream!

Here are some examples of a big dream brainstorm session:

- I will be earning $100,000 per year in 5 years.

- I will be known in my community as the nutrition professional in my specialty that everyone turns to when a presentation or newspaper interview is necessary.

- I have a full private practice, incorporating private, one-on-one clients, presentations and consulting for corporations.

- I have four contractors who see personal training clients on a full-time basis.

- I personally work three days per week, but have five professional contractors working for me who each have full, 40-hour workloads.

- I spend much of my free time mentoring others in the community, exercising, focusing on self-care, reading and gardening, and spending time with family and friends.

- I am a nationally sought-after speaker, for topics of my specialty, limiting my speaking travel to no more than 4 times a year.

- I have created a vesting formula for contractors who stay with the company, so that I will retire in 20 years, allowing one or more contractors to take control of the company.

- I travel no less than 5 weeks per year for enjoyment.

- I attend no less than 3 national conferences and various educational workshops for professional improvement.

Three scenarios to consider

Exercise 1.3

I encourage you; if you want to get the most out of this book, stop right here and work on this exercise. Answer these three questions:

1.   You are witnessing an event celebrating your birth 200 years into the future. Everyone you have ever known or who has ever heard of you will be there to dedicate a fountain to you. What are the people saying about you?

2.   There is a huge billboard along the freeway or main highway in your area. You can put anything you want on it to promote your business. What does it look like and what does it say?

3.   Who are you dedicated to in making a difference?

The purpose of this exercise is to help you determine a life purpose statement. Yes, it will take more than just these questions to get you there, and in Chapter 6, you will delve into this more deeply, but these questions will start you thinking about why you are on this earth and what impact you want to make while you are here.

To provide you with an example, my life purpose is to make a difference in people's lives who dream of starting their own business. They are afraid, though. They think people will laugh at them. So, at my dedication are people whose great-great grandparents started a business that has since grown and served as an example to their generation that anything IS possible.

My billboard shows my corporation logo of two people on a mountain, one helping the other reach for the stars, and telling readers that anything is possible. I am dedicated particularly to men or women who want their own business more than anything they can imagine but are scared to death to try. Yet they can trust me to take them by the hand and help them pull that inner strength from within themselves to really make it all happen!

Who you must be to make it happen

So now you may have a better idea of what you would really like to create! This is a good time to address that if you believe it to be so, you CAN make it happen! Adjust your mindset: You no longer are THINKING about creating an incredible business, you ARE creating it! And, you can see it in your mind. So, start sharing your vision with others. In fact, that is your next assignment!

Exercise 1.4

Pick no fewer than 5 people you know. Share the business you plan to create and what your vision is for that business. Before you begin, write down to whom you will tell. This will help make it happen. Put the list of what you would like to achieve in your e-book or notebook. Then come back to that list and make notes for what they say when you tell them. THEN write down your feelings about what they just told you.

Something you have to remember is that you will soon need to be able to ask people for business. Successful business professionals are where they are partially because they were not afraid to ask for the business! So although we will address this in later chapters, I am warning you now that this will be part of the person you will need to become in order to create the business of your dreams. Consider it like the effort in building up new muscle – right now you may shudder at the thought of asking for business, but with practice, you'll get better, and maybe even GOOD at it!

It is now time to address creating the person you have to be to make your vision happen! You have taken a huge step in writing it down and a bigger step sharing it, but it will take more than that to turn your vision into reality. And we haven't even made it to the planning yet! If I tossed the planning phase to you now, you would give up . . . probably much like the manner in which you have in the past.

Moving into Reality

There are four steps to moving yourself into the 'reality' stage:

1. A commitment to make it happen.

Your commitment must start in your heart. You have to believe something can happen before you will actually take action to make it reality. Ask yourself what kind of person you are when it comes to commitment: Are you willing to commit 100% and do what it takes? Starting a successful business *is* hard work!

The commitment must be complete in order to achieve your goal, however. Some people start working towards a goal, but when things get tough, they cut and run. Or they continue to take tentative steps, but not really commit. Often this action has more to do with a person's own confidence in what he or she can accomplish than with his/her level of commitment. If that is the case, and if a person wants it badly enough, he or she can seek help from a coach to help him or her work through those limiting internal conversations.

Kathleen had spent years trying to get her business up and running. She had actually started – and stopped – working with me several times. When things would get rough, she would give up and go back to "finding a job." But she also had a lot of personal trauma going on in her life, which made it particularly difficult to focus on starting a business. However, she was eventually able to resolve her personal life issues and began the process of building her business again.

Although things again became tough, this time Kathleen was able to work through the limiting conversations and consider the pros and cons to sticking with the process to make her dreams come true. Today she has her website up, has sales from her site coming in, has a contract with a local school system, and is starting to see private clients. It's been a long, hard process, but she is now seeing the fruits of all those struggles.

When committing to something, however, this also means that something else must be given up. Consider what you would give up if you were to start your own business, or to grow it into what you really dream of. It may be time with your family and friends, as you first develop your business and then work endless hours to get it up and running successfully. You may give up security such as insurance benefits and pay from your "day job." And, ultimately, you may mortgage your home or take out a personal or SBA loan to get your business up and running, risking your personal credit and assets. It is important for everyone starting a business to realize they may have to commit finances that put them out of their comfort zone. Each person must determine how far he or she can go.

Samantha came to me to start her new business. She had moved to a new state and had decided to take the plunge. This was huge because Samantha was single and currently living off of her savings. She knew she wanted to secure a Small Business Administration (SBA) loan, so we specifically worked on helping her create the all-important business plan. It took about 8 months, but today she has her SBA loan and her business is starting to take off!

It's not always because a person isn't committed that leads to avoiding a dream or ending prematurely. Sometimes it may have more to do with believing in themselves and knowing that they really can accomplish anything if they want it badly enough. I will often ask clients how they will feel if they do not strive for this goal, and as they ponder the alternative, they become stronger in their resolve and more confident that they can achieve their goal.

Exercise 1.5

On a scale of 1-10, how committed are you? Write down what you are willing to risk and what you are NOT willing to risk.

2. Do what you are passionate about.

This is huge! Without passion, commitment will be harder to maintain. Desire determines destiny. If your desire is strong enough, you will accomplish what you dream of. Passion will increase your willpower. It helps fuel your commitment. If you follow your passion, you become more dedicated to your goal, and when you allow your passion to come out when interacting with others, you will find that others pay closer attention to you. People love passion and it can be contagious, drawing people to you. With your business, you have to identify exactly what you are passionate about and be sure that is your focus with your business. You will be working on this in future sections of the book.

Mike had started his business about a year before coming to me. He was now ready to quit his part-time job and go into his business full-steam-ahead. And he was excited that his marketing to therapists and doctors in the area was producing results! However, as he worked through the process of identifying his ideal client, he started to stall. At first he thought he was SURE who his ideal clients were, but he was beginning to have doubts! With much soul-searching, he realized that this population he had been working with, and did have a talent with, was *not* his ideal client after all! Once he was able to see this and accept it, his progress proceeded forward with renewed vigor.

Exercise 1.6

Make a list of all the things about a prospective business that incite passion within you and then look at your list. If you had to pick just ONE of those things, what would it be?

This may be very hard to answer right now, but stop and consider all the things you love to do and write them down. If you had to do one thing all day, every day, what would it be? Do you prefer variety? If so, what *things* would you like to do on a regular basis? Don't worry if you really don't know. You will be coming back to this question in later chapters. Write *some* ideas down, though.

3. Keep your eye on the goal.

For anything to succeed, you have to have an end in sight. You have to know what the goal is. This helps you create your plan. As Stephen Covey says in his book, *7 Habits of Highly Successful People*, you have to have the end in sight in order to succeed. Again, what is your vision? What do you ultimately want to create? This may sound like a simple question, but once I start pushing clients to really answer this, they find they aren't as sure as they previously thought. I suspect this is why they never took action towards that dream! Once you are clear about what you want to accomplish, then you can create the plan to help you get there and the strategies to move forward. Writing down your goals, identifying the steps necessary to achieve them, and creating an action plan all help you check to be sure that you are still on track in achieving your goal. Again; how can you get there if you don't know where "there" is?

Exercise 1.7

Write down some of your top goals you would like to accomplish with your business. Consider three-month goals, six-month goals, and 1-year goals for now. You'll be coming back to this, but this exercise will get you started in thinking about these issues.

4. Let your courage shine through.

Stepping out of your comfort zone and facing your fears is a trait that can make the difference between success and failure. Remember I mentioned the trait of tolerance of risk as an entrepreneur? Everyone has fears about something. The difference between those who succeed and those who just dream is what they do with that fear. We all have a choice: Face the fear or run from it. The most common action is to run from it.

Some may call facing up to your fears courage. Courage begins with an inward battle. Who will win that limiting conversation you will have with yourself? Are you willing to step up and face those fears? Courage is having the power to let go of the familiar and forge ahead into new territory. Courage is the willingness to put it all on the line for possible failure. Many of the top leaders in the world have suffered failures. They say that those who succeed the most also have suffered the most failures in their lives. But imagine the feeling of success, and also consider how you will feel if you allow your fears to tame your dreams and allow yourself to look back at your life with just dreams to think about.

One of the fears many new entrepreneurs will face is how they will pay for a new business. Before we more deeply address fears, it is important to take a short journey into how you can finance a start-up business if you don't have any outside funding. For many people, they think there is just no way – however...turn the page and enter the world of bootstrapping.

Review of Chapter 1:

✓ What would you do if there were no fear of failure?

✓ Determine what your life dream is

✓ Determine your level of commitment

CHAPTER 2

How to Use "Bootstrapping" to Start Your Business

None of us got where we are solely by pulling ourselves up by our bootstraps. We got here because somebody - a parent, a teacher, an Ivy League crony or a few nuns - bent down and helped us pick up our boots.

– Thurgood Marshall

When I started my business, I used a free online nutrition analysis program. I would enter the client's information into the program, get the results, then copy and paste them into a file that had my letterhead on it. I also used my accountant's version of Quickbooks for many years until I decided it was time to invest in my own copy. These are two examples of waiting until I could afford it to spend money on supplies or software.

When you begin a business, one of the most limited resources will be cash. Bootstrapping is the process of finding out how to get things done without having to borrow - it's the ultimate in creativity! Eventually, however, in order to *really* grow your business, you will have to expand beyond what most of us can accomplish through bootstrapping. However, since we're addressing the initial start-up, seeing clients, and generating money now, I think it's important to address this topic as a chapter all by itself.

I am probably the queen of bootstrapping. Call it power, call it being in control, call it wanting to know it all. Regardless of the motivation, the most enjoyable thing for me has been to figure out how to do something with as little cash outlay as possible. I started my original company, MEG Fitness, with just my time. I was even able to promote my services by writing a free weekly health column and then took advantage of a cheaper alternative to advertising in another newspaper by being featured in its health section. All it takes is desire and a bit of creativity. There are tons of articles on bootstrapping and multiple books on the subject.

When I think of the term bootstrapping, I always think of starting a business without outside financial help, but technically, it means "using a special process to perform a task that one would be unable to do in general." I found that it *can* refer to much more than just business! But for our purposes, I am referring to the term as I have always considered it – raising yourself, and your business, up by your own bootstraps.

One of my personal training clients is the epitome of bootstrapping success. He never borrowed to grow his business, which now generates sales of over $500,000 a year. He worked hard, did without until he had to have something or someone else, and has been very conservative with his growth and business goals and objectives.

With any new and small business, especially small health or fitness practices, chances are you are going to start it with the sweat and tears of your own efforts. You may be in a position where you can quit your 'day job' and still pay your bills, but few people are even in a position to do that at first. So, many of you must create the plan and vision for your business, and then get it up and running, part-time and with your own finances. Many people feel this is just too overwhelming a proposition to seriously consider, but I know it can be done, because not only did I do it, but many of my former clients have done it. As the business grows, they have a better chance to secure outside financing, but when creating the idea and the plans, the big key will be to start and grow with as little cash as possible.

In business school, we have learned that there are several sources of funding for starting a business: The first is what is termed "FFF" for Family, Friends and Fools. This category would be where smaller amounts of cash would be offered, maybe $5,000 to $20,000.

The second is finding an "Angel." An Angel is someone with a lot of money who would be willing to invest in your company. Often this is a retired businessperson who has a lot of residual income and is content to put his/her money to work on a high-risk investment. Often an Angel is willing to invest larger amounts of money than the first category. Banks, in the form of a Small Business Association (SBA) loan, are another possible funding source, which actually can be less demanding beyond just making your payments. You may also be able to take out a home equity or small personal loan, as well. However, if they know the money is for your business, banks generally want to see a comprehensive business plan that will outline how you will be able to make your loan payments while growing your business.

The final funding source is from Venture Capitalists (VCs) and VC organizations. VCs usually only consider companies that have large growth and profit potential. They are looking for that company that will likely go public or sell for an incredible profit and provide an amazing return on their investment.

Now you know of possible funding sources, and you probably don't have a rich uncle or father, you don't know any wealthy family friend who wants to lend money to you, and you're not ready for an SBA loan or VC funding. The fact is that 99.9% of all business owners will pull their business up by their own "bootstraps." That probably means you! Let's now look at how you can make it happen with what you have:

Focus on your cash flow, not profits. This is an old lesson in schools of business. Reality is you have to pay your bills, so the biggest motivation is on sales. For a service business, this means bringing in clients! There are multiple stories of companies who grew to success all based on those first customers and clients. Then, not only do they have cash coming in, but they also have a source of referral for new clients! For this reason, my ultimate goal for new clients is to help them get past the stage of planning and actually put the word out there that they are open for business. This is a scary time for many. What if you fail? The bigger question is; "What if you don't try?"

Just do it! What this means is that, as I mentioned earlier, many of my clients like to plan, plan, plan, and the last thing they want to do is get out there and do it! But you can't make money by planning only! No matter how well you plan, until you start working with clients, you won't know what works and what does not work. Granted, you do have to plan, but no matter how much planning you do now, you will change procedures and processes as your experience grows. You can't build up experience if you don't start seeing clients.

So, let's discuss some options to actually get things going. Here are some suggestions to move you into generating interest in your services, now:

1. If potential clients use the Internet, which many do, **do you have a website yet?** If not, it's time to create one. For less than $200 and a weekend's worth of time, you can get a 3-page website up and running in no time. And you don't have to know html, either! For more details on how to set up a website on your own, see the companion e-book.

2. **Contact your local newspaper** and, with samples in hand, meet with the editor to propose writing a weekly column on a topic of interest to you. Some papers today use articles available through

databases now, instead of local talent, but if you offer your services for free, and they like your work, they may accept your offer. Be sure to always include your contact and bio information at the bottom of each column.

3. **Contact all the local community groups** and offer to speak. Many clubs and organizations, such as the local Rotary Club, are always looking for speakers who are willing to volunteer their time.

4. **Contact your local library** to see if they make rooms available for workshops and presentations. Many offer rooms for no charge.

5. **Contact local supermarkets** to determine interest in offering supermarket shopping tours. Talk to the manager.

6. **Meet with club managers and owners of health clubs** to offer workshops on a topic of interest to either trainers or club members.

Exercise 2.1

1. Write down at least three ideas for how you can promote your services today.

2. Come back to your list and write down the results of your attempts and then the results of the activity.

Keep your day job. Many of you will have to keep your full-time or part-time job while creating your business. The best way to keep the pressure off is to know you still have a regular income. That way, you aren't motivated by panic and can clearly define what your goals and vision are and create the plans to make it happen. It depends on your level of risk tolerance, however. If you have a substantial savings, or income and support from a significant other, you may prefer to quit your job and immerse yourself into the research and planning necessary to make your business a success now. It can happen! But first, determine financial goals you would like to achieve and by when you would like to achieve them. Perhaps an initial goal would be to generate $300/week, which would be the sign to start negotiating going to part-time in your job. A second goal might be for $500/week, at which time you will give your notice, if that's sufficient for your needs.

This is a good time to mention something important that can affect various employees. Some of my clients have been bound to employee agreements that do not allow them to start up their own business on the side. Be sure to check your employee agreement to find out what your rights are as an employee. For more details on this topic, see the companion e-book.

Get your name out there. Sometimes the best way to become known in your community is by offering free presentations or workshops. Just showing up at various events can quickly create awareness of your services. Examples include health fairs, school fairs, chamber events or community events such as bike races or marathons. Attend lunches and networking events and offer to give small presentations on your area of expertise. This is one of the easiest forms of free advertising.

Exercise 2.2

1. Write down at least four ways you will attempt to get your name out into the community.
2. Come back and write down the results of that attempt or activity.

You can do most of it on your own. In order to build a large business, there is big emphasis on building a team, but this can take several years. If you are looking at conserving as much of your funds as possible, there are always ways to do it yourself or only contract out for services that either will take too long to learn or you just have no interest in doing. For years I used templates to create my own websites. I studied all I could on Search Engine Optimization (SEO) and how best to create a website, learning about website text, white space, headers and sub-headers, etc. Until business was so busy that I could no longer justify the time I spent working on my websites, I was content to do it all myself.

Other examples of doing it on your own are creating your own business cards, flyers and brochures. Most of us have the necessary software on our computers to create each of these promotional tools. All you need is a printer and ink, and you can have your own business card printed in no time. And, as details of your business change, such as adding a business phone line, a website or new office location, you can easily change your cards without having to throw out cards you spent several hundred dollars on. It's very important to keep track of your budget, however, so don't start spending a lot of money you don't have, before you have it.

Focus on function. You imagine that perfect office or location, but you have an extra room in your house. If you want to start making money now, use what you have! When you have more money, you can then invest in a better location. The key is to see clients now, not wait until you can have the ideal setting. You may also wonder what is the best computer software program to help you work with clients, but often there are free or cheap options available online that will meet your needs. Don't let such details hold you back from starting! Remember that Bill Gates started in his garage!

Forecast. I always ask clients how much money they would like to make in their first year, but then I have them break it down. How many clients would they like to see each week? Then we determine how much they will need to charge for each client and each situation to determine how they will meet that goal income. Many individuals undervalue their services.

Another part of forecasting is to know what your expenses are. If you have no understanding of how much you're spending on your business, you can end up out of business before you've even started, so again, I emphasize determine a budget in advance and stay within that budget.

Because my clientele are very careful and conservative, this has never been an issue with any of them, but you have to keep in mind that you can't spend more than you are taking in or have to invest in your business. For this reason, not only is it imperative to start seeing clients immediately and that you keep your expenses down, but it's also critical that you understand what your current expenses are and how they will grow as the business grows. As you progress through your business plan, track what increased expenses you might experience with different scenarios of growth. Many clients use an Excel spreadsheet that helps them determine forecasted cash flows.

Start with what you know. Let's say you dream of opening up a health and fitness spa, but you want to start your business now, and you also enjoy working with people with food sensitivities. Creating a spa will take outside funding and a lot of market research, but seeing clients individually or in groups right now will just take some marketing and getting your name out there. As you work on your business plan, think of the ultimate vision and set up the steps to make that happen. While working with clients, you can also start conducting the research necessary for the ultimate goal of a thriving health and fitness spa.

Tristen wanted to start a business that would incorporate her functional nutrition education. However, she used this skill very seldom, because she worked for a diabetes center most days, and then one day a week consulted for a functional medicine doctor, seeing perhaps three clients a week using her functional nutrition skills. When she started to do her research on what was necessary to get her business up and running, she hit a major roadblock. She didn't feel she had enough skills to work with this type of client on her own yet. It was a hard struggle to continue to move forward. However, a new opportunity came forth of providing weight loss classes to older women. This was a service that felt very easy to her, so although her functional nutrition practice is on hold, at least she is now moving forward again!

Always say yes! I know this is a scary proposition, but suppose your vision is to provide corporate health programs to local organizations and a company calls you today and say they would love to have YOU create a wellness program for their company. They would like you to start it in 2 months, they want all 100 employees involved, you can create as many groups as you like from those 100 people, and they are offering you your asking rate for not only the time you will spend in presenting the program but also for creating it. The first emotion you experience is amazement that it's actually happening, then utter fear, and then panic sets in. BUT; you say yes! You cannot afford to say you'll get back to them! This is increased cash flow AND it answers that question, "Does this help me achieve my goals, now?" with a yes.

One first theory in business is always saying yes and THEN figure out how you'll get it done (as long as it answers the question, 'does this help you achieve your goal, now?' with a yes). But, again, you must quickly assess if a proposition helps you achieve your goals, now.

I have had many clients who have such opportunities fall in their lap, and they still say no, although it's exactly what they want. They just don't yet feel ready! However, if you trust yourself, there are an unlimited number of options and resources available to you when you allow your creativity to come into play. It's funny how creative we become when fear of failure drives us and the passion to make it really happen motivates us.

Emphasize what makes you unique. You don't have the luxury of comparing yourself with the leaders of your industry when you're starting out on a shoestring. You must draw clients/customers to you by focusing on yourself, period. Emphasize your unique brilliance and what brings out your passion. Why will a client come to you instead of sign up for a hospital-based weight loss program? Why will they call you for your personal training services instead of joining the health club? It has to be more than money; it has to be something about you and the unique services or care you offer. When you don't have the fancy trimmings to attract clients, you have to fall back on what you do have to offer and use that as your competitive edge.

If you have a dream to start your business, don't let lack of funds stop you in your tracks. The number of successful entrepreneurs who have grown a thriving business from nothing is huge! Life is too short to live in a dream of what might have been.

Now that you have a few ideas of how you can actually get your business up and running, it's time to next address those limiting conversations floating around in your head.

Review of Chapter 2:

✓   Understand what bootstrapping is

✓   Determine how much you must do on your own to start your business

✓   Decide on affordable strategies you can do now

CHAPTER 3

Fears, Doubts and Limiting Conversations

Dealing with the Voices in Your Head

"You gain strength, courage and confidence by every experience in which you really stop to look fear in the face... You must do the thing you think you cannot do."

Eleanor Roosevelt

I equate what my clients go through with learning how to fly or hang glide. They are standing at the edge of a great canyon, looking down into a huge valley. I am asking them to jump and trust that they can fly. Like baby birds, learning to spread their wings. They have to learn to trust themselves and trust that they really can do anything they can imagine!

Sam called me a couple of years ago because he knew he wanted to start his own business. But he didn't quite feel ready. In our conversation, he was able to determine what steps he needed to take to GET ready. A year later he called and said, "I'm ready". Today he has a thriving studio and has overcome his fears and those limiting conversations he was having with himself.

What do you do with the fear?

Does fear stop you from striving for something you dream of doing? For some people, fear paralyzes them into inaction and appears as real as their reflection in the mirror. I'm here to tell you that even that reflection isn't always reality.

FEAR is:

F = False

E = Expectations

A = Appearing

R = Real

When I talk to clients for the first time who dream of starting their own business, the most prevailing emotion I hear, above that of hope, is fear. This is extremely common. When asked about their fears, they admit that they are afraid that they will fail, that people will laugh at them, that they will not be viewed as credible professionals worthy of attention or no one will want what they have to offer. There is another fear that can pop up, which is the fear of success.

First, this is our own perception of what 'reality' is. Second, what you DO with that fear can make the difference between a career of your dreams or looking back at your life with regret. Until we are really clear about what it is we want to do, it is hard to envision it being real, and the unknown is a very scary place. The clients who decide to work with me are the people who have a desire for their dreams that is stronger than their fear, and they are able to allow themselves to take a chance; I have never heard any of them complain that they had taken that chance.

Meredith had called me because she wanted her own business desperately. But I didn't hear back from her.... Until a year later. She admitted her extreme fear that she would make a fool out of herself if she failed, but she wanted it so badly that she was now willing to risk that failure. We often discuss the tether that is holding onto her ankle, but at least now she is practicing flying! I am still working with her, and even with that continuing fear, she is moving forward and has started seeing clients now! And she has other contracts for other projects. We continue to work on the fears, using some of the tools mentioned below.

How to overcome the fear

First, you must really face the fears. Ignoring them will not make them go away; they will just linger, to raise their ugly heads (as with a two-headed monster) at times when the going is really getting tough. It's the fears that paralyze us. Although this is where the assistance of a coach can really help you, you can also start this work on paper by yourself. If you find yourself hitting a brick wall, however, contact someone to help you.

What is the cost of not doing what you are most afraid to do? Examples of cost is working at a job you dread, feeling like you are missing something you are meant to do in your life. Another example is really enjoying your days. People avoid doing what they most dream of because usually they are most afraid they will lose everything they own. Sure, that is always possible, but when you really consider this, and you think back to the last chapter where you had to write down how committed you are, would you really risk losing EVERYTHING? Chances are the answer is no.

Exercise 3.1

Answer these questions:

1. Define the worst thing that could happen if you did what you are considering. Write this all down in detail, every dreadful thing. Then rate the permanent impact it would have on a scale of 1-10.

2. What steps could you take to repair the damage above?

3. What are the beneficial outcomes of taking the step in #1? Rate it on a scale of 1-10.

4. What are you putting off due to fear?

5. What is the cost of putting this off?

The next step in starting the path towards that dream is to set up goals. Sound familiar? We will come back to this in more detail in the next chapter. If you don't know where you're going, how do you plan to get there? We wouldn't dream of driving to a location without knowing how to get there, so why would we assume it's any different with a business or career plan?

In the meantime, though, start with a small goal, one that isn't as scary as the big, big goal. Perhaps your big dream is to become a famous author. You don't even know if you can write! So, a simpler goal would be to start writing small, easy articles for online article submission sites. Failure with this is not an option; the sites will accept articles on any topics. A few examples of article submission sites include:

GoArticles.com, http://www.goarticles.com

EzineArticles.com, http://www.ezinearticles.com

Alumbo.com, http://www.alumbo.com.

Spend some time on these to see what they offer and how you can submit articles. This will also help draw traffic to your website. So, that smaller goal might be that you will write one article and submit it to the above three article submission sites.

Another example of breaking a BIG dream into smaller steps would be, if you dream of becoming a public speaker, offer to speak to a local community group on a topic of interest to the public. And join Toastmasters International, today! Your first goal could be that you will join Toastmasters.

A third example would be that you would like to make a million dollars a year. So, break it down; maybe consider how much you would like to make in the next three to six months. That first goal could be that you will be generating $X/month from your business in the next three months.

A final example might be that you would just like to get your business up and running and quit your job! A good first step may be to complete this book.

Exercise 3.2

Write down at least one small goal you would seriously like to accomplish right now. Besides writing it down on your e-book or notebook, also write it on a separate piece of paper. Be specific; include details and a deadline. One example would be that you will be generating $300/week in 3 months.

Once you have written your goals, it will suddenly become a little more real. It can take people a long time to even get this much done, however. If the fears are still real, and you continue to struggle with this part, consider how lofty your goals are. Perhaps they are too overwhelming because they are encompassing too large of a time period. If that is the case, create a goal for just the next six months. Ideally you want to look at what you want to create in 5-10 years from now, but if that holds you back, it's still okay to create a 6-month goal.

Mary dreamed of owning a thriving business, but she was still struggling with what that would look like. She continued to research and research and research. This is a common tactic when someone is very fearful. Although writing was not her goal, in order to help move her forward, one day I challenged her to write an article on the topic of her greatest passion. She didn't want to actually commit to the entire article at first, but she was willing to create an outline. From there she then put a completed article together. Her next assignment was to determine where to send that article, which was to various article submission sites. Today she is finally building that business of her greatest passion and dreams.

Another effective strategy for some people is to verbally tell yourself you have already accomplished your goals every morning. Wake up and tell yourself you have a thrilling, thriving private nutrition practice or personal training/fitness business and just love going to work each day. Tell yourself that you have the dream job of your life and can't believe how lucky you are. The more you tell yourself what you *want* to be real, the more likely you will *create* that reality. Okay, I can hear you now; I agree that just telling yourself you have the life you want won't make it happen. However, what it WILL do is help you believe that it's possible and motivate you to work on setting up the structure to make it real.

Exercise 3.3

To take that strategy a step further, next write down your goal on sticky notes and put them in various locations that you will see daily, such as in your car, in your daily planner, and on your bathroom mirror. Write down that goal as if it has already happened.

One example would be to write down on your note, "I am generating $300/week and it feels GREAT!" As you continue to KNOW it will happen, along with the plans and strategies you create, the more likely it is that you will turn that 'wish' into reality.

What do you believe?

If you still struggle with coming up with goals, you need to determine and resolve your limiting beliefs and address your fears. They will not go away by themselves, and if you are reading this book because you have been 'thinking' about starting your own business for years, all of that thinking may be due to those beliefs and fears that have held you back from actually taking action.

What do you honestly believe you can do? Sure, everyone has doubts about what is possible for them. These beliefs, however, are what will hold you back if you are sure, in your mind, that you cannot accomplish your dreams. Often my clients start working with me with strong doubts that they can really create a thriving business, but a stronger desire to TRY. And, by the end of our work together, their beliefs in what they can do has totally changed and they now know they can do anything they can imagine.

Exercise 3.4

Write down your list of beliefs, good and bad. If you find one you do not really *want* to believe, that will be the one (or ones) to focus on below. Next, below that belief, write down what you want your belief to be.

Exercise 3.5

Follow these steps:

1. Write down your limiting belief. One example may be that you just don't know enough to really attract your ideal clients.

2. Now write down what you want you really do want to believe. Using the above example, you know more than the average population and are an expert in your field. Once you start working with people, you will be so busy you will have to either hire someone, book clients way into the future, or find a better way to see more people at a time.

3. Now ask yourself if your original belief is really true? Can you absolutely KNOW it is true?

4. When you think of this limiting belief, how do you feel or react? For example, do you feel a lump in your throat, a pain in your gut? Do you feel tired or depressed? What images come up when you think of that limiting belief?

5. Now ask yourself what does it cost you to have that belief? What I mean by 'cost' is what do you not do because of that belief? One cost may be fewer clients because you don't believe you know how to market yourself.

6. Now, who would you be without that belief? Using the above example, you may be a successful businessperson who has just the right wording and feelings to attract your ideal clients.

7. Then ask yourself how you BENEFIT from this limiting belief? Don't say you don't. There's some payoff you get from having this belief. Perhaps it's by staying safe, or avoiding the risk and disappointment if it starts to take off and then dies, or perhaps you're even avoiding success!

8. Now it's time to turn around that stated belief. For example, you do know much more than your clients do, who will value the information you can provide them with.

9. How is this turnaround as true as the original belief, or more true? Don't just go through the motions; imagine your turnaround belief and walk through the scenario where potential clients are actually calling you and you are providing information that they didn't know.

10. Write down your action steps to make it a new belief. Examples would include attending education seminars, speaking to community groups, reading books on the topic of your passion and interest, getting help such as consultants and coaches to move you forward.

If you did the work above, were you able to identify and resolve some limiting conversations and fears? If not, work on more limiting conversations and perhaps contact a coach to help move you forward.

Candy is just one example of a client who would stop in her tracks because she would suddenly feel that she just didn't know enough to really work with clients. She felt she wasn't ready because she wasn't an 'expert'. However, as she continued to work through her limiting conversations, she was logically able to see that she knew much more than her average clients, and as she jumped in, her confidence grew. She saw her value and that people valued her expertise. For some people this is a very hard process that takes a long time to work through. It has taken Candy almost a year to get over these limiting conversations.

A word about passion

Some people come to me because although they already have a successful business, they are not enjoying what they do or they are not seeing the growth they had originally envisioned. They have all the 'technical' pieces in place, but what they have failed to do is investigate what their passion is!

All of us must clearly define what it is we love to do in order to be successful at it. Without passion, we will not convey the message to potential clients or employers that we are good at what we do. Without enjoying the activity we have in mind, we won't give it our all.

You know it when you are talking about your passion or when you're just going through the motions. Here is your next assignment:

Exercise 3.6

Think of two subjects – one you are passionate about and one that really bores you. Then find someone who is willing to hear you talk about both. Don't tell them what you're doing in advance.

Spend about 5-10 minutes talking about each subject. After you have talked about both subjects, ask the person to share what they observed. Write down what you learn in your notebook.

Fear of success: Just as real

As I progress with clients, though, there is another fear that starts to show its ugly face: The fear of success. This is not just a female trait; I have seen it in male clients, as well. Men just don't talk about it as easily as women do. Fear of success is just as paralyzing as fear of failure but may show up later in the process of building the business. It may even be more paralyzing, though, because these are deeper-held beliefs.

> Dan was slowly building up an empire, but something was continuing to hold him back. As we delved deeper into the issue, we discovered that Dan was gravely afraid of becoming something different once he 'made it'. He was afraid he would become aloof and lose his friends and his family would no longer care to be around him.

These really are very common fears.

Do you wonder about these questions? If so, you may have a fear of success:

- What if you accomplish your dreams but find you still are not happy?

- What if you are more successful than others who are so much smarter than you?

- What if you become someone you no longer like or that people will no longer like you for who you are inside?

- What if your success leads to the loss of those you love?

- What if the success is suddenly gone, just when you start to enjoy how it feels?

Part of these fears has to do with a lack of self-confidence and doubt that have helped keep you in your comfort zone for years. It's the creation of the self-fulfilling prophecy that 'I can never really make it big'. These fears show up through sudden lack of organization, indecision, procrastination and lack of motivation. However, just becoming aware of this fear can help resolve it because then you can create a strategy to address and resolve these issues.

As with ways to address fear of failure, there are also effective strategies to help work through fears of success. First of all, you can go back to the earlier exercise to address your limiting conversations. Meanwhile, also practice these strategies:

- Visualize what your life will look like when you achieve these goals of success. This will help you keep things in perspective.

- Never allow yourself to be okay with excuses. This will force you to face your fears.

- Continue to monitor your level of commitment and motivation to reach your goals. Have you slowed down or are you putting off some of your action steps?

- When you achieve a milestone in working towards your goals, acknowledge those successes you have achieved. There may be others whom you can acknowledge in your journey, too.

- Be sure to continually request those in your life to constantly give you honest, open, candid feedback when they see you backsliding or self-destructing.

- Learn how to accept compliments and recognition from others.

- It is important that creating this new dream encompasses all aspects of happiness in your life and has not been created as a way to escape something else in your life.

James and Constance Messina (Ph.D.s) have an exercise on Coping.org (http://www.coping.org/growth/success.htm) that can take you deeper into addressing your fears of success.

Another fear to address is the fear of what wealth may bring to you. To address your "financial set point" and how to overcome it, T.

Harv Eker challenges you to learn how to re-set your set point and learn to accept success and great financial wealth in his book, *Secrets of the Millionaire Mind*.

Controlling the fears

In 1996, it didn't even dawn on me to be fearful of starting my own small business. Sure, I wondered if it would be successful and if I would meet my initial business goals, but I also knew that there was no other option for me to choose; it was just the right thing for me at that moment. My initial goal was achieved in 1.5 years and I have never looked back. I just look forward, towards the possibilities I know are always there, available for the asking. Today I am taking my business higher than I ever imagined back then. But it takes risk!

When you allow fear to control what you will do with your career and life, you will eventually look back at your life with regret. We live for such a short period of time on this planet that it's a shame if we don't strive for the things we dream of doing. If there is anything in your life that you have dreamed of, but have still not made an attempt, I challenge you to step outside your comfort zone and make that dream a reality. Doing this in just little ways can help you set the stage for bigger things in the future. Allow your fear of NOT doing it become a higher priority than the fear of trying and failing.

There's the reality; it's in your mind. If you know something can happen, it will happen. And, with that in mind, let's go onto the next step of helping you create your goals.

Review of Chapter 3

✓   Steps for overcoming fear

✓   Working through limiting conversations

✓   Discovering your passions

✓   Investigating fear of success

CHAPTER 4

Goals

"A goal without a plan is just a wish."

–Antoine de Saint-Exupery (1900 – 1944)

It's not uncommon for new clients to really have no idea what they want to create. Joanna was pretty typical. She knew she wanted a business, but by the simple questions I asked her during our initial conversation, she realized she hadn't thought much through past the thought of, "I want to work for myself." She had been attending different workshops and reading various books on how to start a business, so she knew she did need to create a business plan, but every time she got to that part, she got hung up and put the plan, and the dream, away.

Even though she wasn't sure she was 'ready', she did want to investigate the reality of starting a business, to at least see if that really *was* her dream. As we started working through the exercises, though, she became more and more excited. She was a great planner and organizer, so approaching a concept that at first seemed vague to her suddenly started to take on form, which propelled her forward. Today she has her own business providing sports nutrition counseling to athletes, teaching at the university, and doing some personal training in a small club where she collaborates with the owner on other programs through the year.

Everyone starts to envision goals when they imagine what they would like their businesses to look like. You may be in a position where you have been considering starting your own business, or you may have a business but are ready to take it to the next level, but for one reason or another have been putting off the steps necessary to 'go there'. You have to set goals to make it reality, however. Often fear is what holds us back from setting goals. What if you fail? Or what if you succeed?? You want it but it scares you terribly!

Less than three percent of all Americans have their goals written down. Eight out of 10 businesses fail within the first 3 years because a surprising number begin their business without creating any plans.

They say that if you don't plan out your journey, you can't get there. If you envision your business going somewhere, how do you know where 'there' is without that plan written down? Another saying is 'Failure to plan is a plan for failure'. But if you never set up your plan, you can't fail, right? However, then you will look back at your life, 20-40 years from now and find yourself saying, 'I wish I had...'

Life is too short to allow yourself to limit your possibilities.

I believe that we all really can achieve anything that we believe is possible. We need to plan for those dreams, however, and be realistic. Just thinking about them will not make them reality, and just opening the doors and saying we're in business will not make our dreams a success. As I've said earlier, we create our own reality, whether that's success or failure, based on the research and work we are willing to put into making those goals happen. What do YOU want to achieve?

Goal-Setting tips

Many people are familiar with SMART goals: This stands for:

S - Specific
M- Measurable
A - Attainable
R - Realistic
T - Timely.

Let's consider some tips to help you create and achieve your goals and create the business of your dreams:

1. Challenge yourself with big goals

Often we need support to think big. Most people tend to set goals that are easy, because they are afraid of failing, but you really can achieve anything; it just may need more planning and time than you initially considered. This is one of the benefits of setting up goals and working on plans to make them happen. As you create your business and marketing plans, you are able to tell if your goals can be accomplished within the time frame you envision initially. If you make your goals too big, you can't realistically achieve them. But if you make them too small, they become de-motivating. The best rule of thumb is to make them challenging but realistic – just a bit uncomfortable but challenging enough to stir up your passion and sense of excitement.

Exercise 4.1

Write down at least three big goals you would like to accomplish in your business. Don't worry about HOW you will make them happen. Just allow yourself to think big and put them in writing.

Janice first came to me with the goal of building a business that would just help her replace her job. However, when we discussed what she would do if there were no fear of failure, one of the things she listed was to write a book. "Why only if there were no fear of failure?" I asked. She replied because it just seemed too big to her. However, as she worked through her business plan, she finally believed that she could put that in her 5-year plan. Now Janice is working on her book!

2. Make your goals specific

I always push my clients to narrow down their goals into exactly what they want to achieve, which helps ensure their success. If your goals are vague, how will you know you accomplished them? How much do you want to make, by when and by doing what? Then you create action steps to achieve these goals. If your goals are specific you are able to measure your progress, but if you have not set up specific goals, what will you measure?

When creating your goals, be sure to have the end in mind. As with a trip, to make it successful, you have to know where your final destination is. If you don't know where you want to go, how will you know when you get there? Then, once you have met that ultimate goal, you will be ready to set new goals.

Exercise 4.2

With the big goals you have written down, look them over to make sure they are specific and make changes if necessary.

3. Cut big goals down to manageable pieces

As mentioned above, you want to think big and challenge yourself. But some goals are huge and need to be broken down into sections so they can realistically be accomplished. Cutting big goals down into multiple smaller goals can help you gradually grow into your larger goal and give you an incredible sense of accomplishment.

If you want to create a business that earns $250,000 a year, and you have no access to outside funding, you may need a few years to make it happen. The first step in breaking down that larger goal is to set up 'secondary' goal(s), such as you will make $30,000 in the first six months from your business. Even as you create your smaller goals, you must then break them down into daily, weekly and monthly goals. Making them this manageable helps you check them off your 'to do' list much more quickly than larger goals. You then get a greater sense of accomplishment, which is very motivating for the next series of goals.

Examples of such smaller goals could be that you will be writing a weekly column for the local newspaper by the end of June and you will have presented to no less than three local community groups by July. Another example is you will complete your business plan and marketing plan in the next month. The point is that these smaller, supplementary goals all help you build your business and name and create the base to a successful business.

Exercise 4.3

In your e-book or notebook, break down one of the big goals that you listed in step 1 into smaller goals. For right now, just pick one of your big goals to narrow down into smaller steps, but be sure to go back and work on them all, later.

4. Share your goals with others

Just writing down the goal and setting it in your mind may not be enough to propel you into action. As a good next step, to ensure you stick with the plan, tell others about your intention. Some clients I work with have not shared their intentions with others. They are staying safe. If they don't tell anyone, if they decide it's too hard, no one will know. However, when this is the case, I challenge them to always pick how many people they will tell. I may have them start small, but the goal is to tell everyone! This shows intention and suddenly the back door has closed – no more escape hatch! Now they HAVE to make it happen!

When I talk to a potential client, I have him or her tell me what his/her three top goals are with the business. For some people, this is the first time they have done this exercise, but for everyone it can be a powerful step to help them share goals that sometimes they have never spoken to another person about. That's one of the tips in accomplishing goals – share your goals with others. In fact, if you share your goals with many people, it does tend to move you forward. Call it fear or call it meeting a challenge that if you failed you would have to live down, but it does work!

Exercise 4.4

Your next exercise is this:

A) First, write down at least five people that you haven't yet told, that you are starting your business. Once you have written your list, look at it. Are these 'safe' people or did you include someone who feels 'scary' to you? You know; someone you would prefer to NOT tell? If they are all safe people, I challenge you to include at least one person to tell who represents stepping out on a ledge.

B) The second part of this exercise is to write a date by which you will tell each person. Then come back and enter the date that you told them.

C) The final part to this exercise is to write down how that experience was for you when you told each person. Again, this may not be a big deal for you, so if that's the case, this may not be a necessary step. If this is a big deal, however, not only write down your feelings, but also feel free to contact me and share!

5. Set a time

One of the hardest things for clients to do is to set time frames for their goals. This really puts meat into what they want to create! They worry about not meeting their time frames. However, as they set up their action plans for their goals, they eventually see what is possible with planning. Putting a time frame to your goals gives you a clear target to work towards. Without a time frame, your goal of 'earn $40,000' could end up a goal you work towards your entire life. In fact, you may relate to this very well, as I have met many people who have created goals without time frames and, years later, are still working on those goals. The number of people I meet who tell me they want to create their own business, but have not done anything about it, is too great to count.

Exercise 4.5

Make sure that each of your smaller goals has a time frame included.

> Josh wanted to start seeing personal training clients on his own. He was tired of working at the health club and felt it was a dead-end job. He had actually told himself earlier that when he finished school that he would really do **something**, but then realized he had been at the club for over a year. When we first spoke, he said he had a goal to make $75,000 a year. He knew other trainers who were self-employed and were making that much, some more! But when I asked him by when he wanted to make that, he had to stop and really think about it. Suddenly just saying it and realizing he had only been giving it lip service was not making it happen. So, in that first conversation, he stepped up and said, "I'd like to be making $75,000 per year in a year from now." NOW we had something to work on!

6. Measure your progress

As mentioned above, when you create your goals, you need to also create a way to measure your progress. You do this so you can tell if a strategy is working or if your goal is as realistic as you initially thought. One example would be that you launch a website and your goal is to attract 1,000 people within three months. You would want to track the number of visitors to see if you were meeting that goal. If not, you would need to make adjustments in order to meet a new goal or achieve that goal.

But a big question people often have is HOW can you measure progress? In order to really properly measure your progress, your goals must meet two important criteria:

1. **Can you quantify the measure?** If you can't put a tangible number or result on it, you can't measure it. You can't measure "empowerment", for instance. But you can measure seeing 2 new clients a week by October. This isn't really different than if you had a client who wanted to lose weight. You would help him determine to how **much** he would like to lose. If he states he would like to lose 50 pounds, then you have a measure you can quantify. If he said he wants to lose enough weight to look better, that would be tougher to measure.

2. **How often will you measure?** You can't just say you want to attract 1,000 people to your website. That could mean anything at any time, such as by the year 2030! Consequently, using the website example, if you indicate that you want to attract 1,000 people to your website within the next three months, you now have two ways to track your progress. First, if you want the resultant outcomes in three months, then you may want to create checking periods. Perhaps you can split the three months up and set a smaller goal as 300-350 visitors by the end of month one, etc. You then want to check your visitors by the end of three months.

Relating this to health, using the above client example, you could help him determine how much time it would take him to lose that chosen amount of weight and set up intermediate testing periods to see if he's staying on track with his ultimate goal.

Exercise 4.6

For your smaller goals you have written down, make sure you have some way to measure your progress, using the examples above.

7. Get support

One great way to move people forward when working on new business goals is by getting support. Everyone who has achieved great success can tell stories of a mentor, coach, colleague or consultant who helped them at various levels of their success. Don't try to go it all alone; everyone needs someone to talk with to share wins, ups and downs, worries and victories and private doubts. That support can come from a business coach, a support or mastermind group, or even from others in a group coaching program, and that support can change with each stage you are in.

Support from others gives the advantage of other perspectives or ideas that may not occur to you. We all need someone to run ideas by, to check to see if we're on track, or to keep us motivated. Family can be a great support, but often family and friends are too close to you to be able to provide an objective outlook to your goals, and strategies you use to accomplish your goals. Family members tend to want to 'fix' things for us, where someone like a coach, professional colleague or group can give ideas or just be an ear to listen to our concerns or thinking process.

Exercise 4.7

List 2-4 people you will ask to be on your support team. Next to their name, enter when you will ask them, and then enter what their answer is.

It can be scary to consider starting a business from scratch. Many people fail because they aren't willing to put in the time, effort and work necessary to understand what is realistic and what they can expect. However, any successful business professional will tell you that, with planning and setting realistic goals, you can create a thriving business. Don't allow fear, uncertainty and self-doubt hold you back from at least taking the steps to investigate creating a business you have been dreaming of for years. Live your life as if this is your only chance to live your dreams. People seldom regret taking chances to enhance their lives, but many people regret not acting on a dream.

As we move forward, there is something important that we must stop to address, which is time management. Turn the page to help you organize the work to come.

Review of Chapter 4:

✓ Setting up goals

✓ Making big goals into small, manageable goals

✓ Measuring goals

✓ Create your support team

CHAPTER 5

Organizing Your Time and Work

"Every day, you exchange a piece of your life for something.
What will you choose to exchange today for?"

Monica Ricci
Professional organizer

It is pointless to go any further without addressing time management and organization, for if you can't control these two important aspects of your life and business, you will continue to struggle, and the struggle may become too much. Often people want to start their own businesses for more freedom, not more stress!

Think about this concept: Effective time management can only begin when you realize and accept that there is no such thing as actually managing time! That phrase assumes that you can 'manage' time. But you can't manage time any more than you can 'manage' the weather. Time continues to move; it's an intangible resource that you can't exactly save for later or store in a box to pull out when you 'have more time'. Yet it is the most valuable resource you have!

At the end of the day, your 24 hours looks just like mine, except the way you managed yourself and your actions determines what you accomplished in those hours. Scheduling, which is allocating time to specific tasks, can help you better manage your time, as can taking specific time-saving actions.

More than a few dozen times, people say to me, 'I don't know how you fit it all in!' Sometimes even *I* don't know how I fit it all in, to be honest. However, not only did I realize early that if I wanted to accomplish the things in my life 'to do' list, I'd better take control of my time. I have learned that time management is a huge issue with many of my clients. So, to help with this common problem, you are going to work through some steps to help you make the most out of your valuable but limited resource: Time.

Map it out

Having many things to do in the course of your day can lead to not getting anything done. We've all been there; we have this small project to complete, another to start, we have to be finished with either by noon to pick up the kids, then of course there is bed and relaxation time. But soon things aren't getting done. Or, we want to start a new project (like start our own business!) and we have no CLUE how we'll fit that in!

Exercise 5.1

Print a schedule that breaks down the day, by the hour, for a whole week. If you have the e-book, there will be a full-sized calendar in there to print up. If you do not have the e-book, there is an example of the calendar in Appendix A. It is also possible to find one online. First shade out the time you sleep, then the time you spend on self-care to get ready for the day and for bed. Then shade out family time; this includes meals, watching movies, helping with homework, etc. If you work, shade that time out, including commuting time. Also include self-care for just you, such as exercise or relaxation time. Then look at the time you have left. You may be amazed at what you find!

One client realized that a HUGE chunk of her time was taken by her part-time job that included a long commute time, which prompted her to consider how she can change that. Once you have mapped out your time, you are then ready to determine what projects are most important and how you will accomplish them. When you have your list of ideas and projects you will actually start working on, you can then look at your available time on your schedule and see when you will have time to work on the business.

Make a list

I could not function through each day without my daily list! Not having my list is like walking into a Williams-Sonoma store without a shopping list. Some people get this feeling from walking into Walmart or Target. It's what walking into a toy store would be like for a kid. There are so many wonderful things to see and do! I write down the tasks that need attending to the next day. Generally my list is related to what I have on my marketing calendar, which helps me organize my entire month. Sometimes, I will create a weekly list, and then break it down from there. Determine what works best for you and put your list together. If you're not used to writing down lists, just start with jotting down a few important things. Maybe you want to make some phone calls tomorrow; write that down. Perhaps you've been meaning to write an article; write it down.

Exercise 5.2

Write down a list of all the things you would like to do, period. Never mind when you would do these things and don't consider any particular time frame right now; we are preparing you for a daily list of things to do. Just write down all your ideas of what you would like to do or what is possible if you really wanted to pursue the opportunity.

Allow yourself to just dream and write down ideas. Maybe you have noticed that the local health club could really use a trainer with your unique talents, or you hear from many people that they would love someone to show them around the supermarket to help them learn how to shop. These are opportunities!

Narrow down your list

I love working with clients in each stage of development, but it is especially exciting working with someone just starting their business. Some call me with no ideas at all, but soon ideas are just flooding their minds. Others come to me with tons of great ideas and incredible opportunities. In fact, they have a HUGE list of what they want to do. Their biggest problem is figuring out how to organize it all and stay focused on what they most want to do, and how to actually make it all happen. It becomes so overwhelming for them that they find themselves doing NOTHING! Now, that defeats the purpose of having such great opportunities at their feet, huh?

You can't do it all, so, you have to narrow down your list of things to do.

> One of the first suggestions I gave to Sue was to create her opportunity list. She actually created a whole opportunity folder! She later told me that it was so empowering, because now she didn't have to worry about missing a great idea or that she would later forget about something that really excited her. She knew that even if she didn't do everything on her growing list, now, she would always be able to come back to it, later, and re-evaluate if it was something she still wanted to do, if it was time to do it, or if it no longer interested her.

Exercise 5.3

Look at your list of ideas in Exercise 5.2 and now mark off the ones that do not answer the question, "Does this help me achieve my goals right now?" This will help you get to the heart of what you really need to pursue and work on right now. The others are great opportunities or projects for later.

These are the basics for the goals and objectives for your business, and are the building blocks for creating your business plan. The business plan is then the basis for building a more comprehensive marketing plan, and the action plans that develop from this. All along the way, you must ask yourself what is most important.

Being most effective with prioritizing

You hear a lot of talk about prioritizing and you likely realize that it basically means put in order what's most important, etc. When people start to think about how best to prioritize, usually the reason is that they want the most results possible out of the time they have available. Prioritizing includes two steps: Determining what needs to be done and deciding on the order in which you will do the tasks. To be most effective, you must weed out the work that does not help you achieve your ultimate goals. You must be able to separate the tasks that need to be done from busywork that eats away at your time. Many of these things can be done less frequently, if at all. Task prioritizing means working on the most important tasks first no matter how tempted you are to get a lot of less essential tasks out of the way.

According to Stephen Covey, in his book, *The 7 Habits of Highly Effective People,* there are four quadrants people generally work in. These include *Important and Urgent, Important and Not Urgent, Not Important and Urgent,* and *Not Important and Not Urgent.* Before I go any further, can you identify your activities that fit into each of these categories? According to Covey, the most effective category to work in is in *Im-*

portant and Not Urgent. When you work in this quadrant, you are not solving problems, you are creating opportunities. If we all worked in this category, it would be the one thing that would have the greatest impact on our life and our effectiveness!

Another way to help prioritize is by looking at an ABC list:

- "A" are activities that ABSOLUTELY must get done, now.

- "B" had BETTER get done soon.

- "C" CAN WAIT for now.

- "D" are activities that can be DELEGATED, but do require follow up.

One trait that many successful business owners share is their ability to prioritize their activities. They do not put off *Important and Not Urgent* activities, and they strive to seldom find themselves in the situation where they are scrambling to meet a deadline. They create a schedule of tasks that fit along the mentioned ABC categories and are able to end their day feeling accomplished and satisfied. It is a trait that can be learned and is one of the important steps to effective time management and business success.

What are some examples for each category? The first one that comes to mind that definitely fits into the "*Not important and not urgent*" category is reading e-newsletters and most email. If you find yourself spending more than perhaps 20-30 minutes a day on these activities and complain you don't have enough time to work on your projects, consider how you can cut those activities down.

An example of something that could fit into "*Not important and urgent*" could be a phone call. You do have a choice when the phone rings! If you are available to talk, when it rings, pick it up. If you are in the middle of an important project that you want to complete by a particular deadline, let it ring! When people feel out of control or victimized, often they do most of their work in this quadrant.

Finally, an example of working in the *"Important and urgent"* quad-rant means you are always allowing things to get in the way of things that were once important but not urgent and are now pressing for last minute completion. You were asked to talk to a group of dietetic students on starting a private practice. This was a wonderful opportunity for you to share your experience with incoming dietitians, and you have had three months to prepare. However, now the talk is tomor-row and you still have no idea what you will say! This is definitely *"Important and urgent"*, yet it didn't have to be.

Look at your values

No matter how frantic life gets, the truly successful people are able to rise above the challenges of short time and pressing deadlines by maintaining their perspectives. What are the things most impor-tant to you? Use your values as your compass to keep yourself on track. Continue to come back to what your ultimate vision is of having that incredibly successful and rewarding business, enjoying the freedoms it offers you.

To give you an example the role value plays, when you created your schedule above, if family and friends are a part of your value system, be sure that while you're working on your business that you are not short-changing time spent with them. If keeping your own health and fitness level optimal is important to you, make sure these activities are included in your schedule and don't allow business to nudge them off the calendar. Where and how you spend your time is part of prioritizing. And this does not mean that your priorities can't change, either. Perhaps a friend needs your time and attention, or your child needs help with homework. You may find that the time you had blocked out for working on a particular project can be put off until the time slot you have open for tomorrow. If you are working in the *Important and Not Urgent* quadrant, you will have more flexibility to do this. This further points out how identifying your values can help you prioritize.

Ramona had started her business before she contacted me. But she was extremely frazzled! The good news was her business was going great! The bad news is she had no plan in place at all, but worst of all was she never had time for her two pre-teen sons. The best tool for her in our work together was the schedule. She was able to determine what days she wanted to see clients at the different physician offices she went to, but she also shaded out the times she wanted to spend with her family. It made all the difference in the world, and the calm that came over her was extremely obvious in later conversations. We then could start focusing on planning the growth and future of her company, rather than how to just keep her head above water.

Achieving goals

When you consider your priorities, you should be considering how each fits into helping you achieve your goals. Your time is precious, so spending time in the less effective quadrants means you're unable to accomplish your goals as quickly as you would like.

Let's again look at a few activities that do NOT fit into this quadrant. As you read these, ask yourself how much time you devote to such activities.

- Reading listserv or bulletin board emails
- Long phone calls
- Reading newsletters
- Taking care of last minute deadlines
- Saying yes to too much

Exercise 5.4

For the next week, keep track of how much time you spend on each of the above activities.

None of these activities help you achieve your goals most effectively. Granted, in order to stay current on important issues related to your business/career, you want to read pertinent newsletters and read what colleagues and potential clients are talking about. And there will always be the occasional last-minute project you have to complete. However, in order to accomplish your high priority goals, all of the above activities must be limited and controlled. This means that perhaps a long phone call can be scheduled and planned, but not interfere with more important items such as creating your business action plans for building your clientele. When you say yes to something, always ask yourself, 'How does this help me achieve my goals right now?' If it doesn't, you can gracefully bow out by just saying, 'I'm sorry, I can't fit it into my schedule right now, but feel free to ask me again in the future,' or something similar.

Many of my clients have this problem; they are afraid they will miss an opportunity when they say no to something. However, they then find themselves unable to take advantage of the opportunities they are most passionate about, because they are over-committed to too many things! If your top goal is to start seeing clients NOW, that's where you must focus your time. If saying yes does not fit into the strategies you have created for accomplishing this goal, then the answer should be no.

The issue of saying no comes up quite often, and the story of Nancy illustrates the power of taking control of saying "No" the best. In our first regular session, we determined that she said "yes" much too often, which was hindering her from having enough time for anything she really wanted to accomplish, including starting a business.

So she started a "No" log. After two weeks, this is what she said about the experience of saying "no", "… I am also realizing current "opportunities" that are hindering my real goals. It is making it easier to plan my "no" responses when I understand why I do not need to say "yes"."

Exercise 5.5

If saying "No" is an issue for you, start a "No" log. Determine how often per week you would like to commit to saying "No" and keep track of your progress for at least a week.

Clean up

"One does not accumulate but eliminate. It is not daily increase but daily decrease. The height of cultivation always runs to simplicity."

–Bruce Lee

Part of what can further clutter your mind and any sense of organization is your physical environment. Where will you work on your business? Do you have a space that allows you to organize your stuff and your mind? Look around your workspace. Is there clutter? Do you have an organized filing system in place?

Did you know that when your work area is cluttered and feeling out of control that YOU feel cluttered and out of control? So, look around and decide where you stand in this area. We've just added something NEW to add to your priority list, however! But the good news is you've also just investigated where you have time to work on projects! So, add this to your priority list and then schedule it into your calendar. However, because this can be overwhelming, pick a specific area you want to work on.

Let's say you live in piles. You would like to eliminate the piles but when you look at them, it's just too much. Just as with a client who wants to lose weight or start an exercise program, but it feels too overwhelming to them, you must break this big project into smaller, manageable tasks. For the piles, you may pick one pile, or you may break a large pile in half and just work on that first half. As you work through the pile, each item you come to put into a separate pile that will represent a file folder for the future. If you save articles on nutrition, you may want to put all the nutrition articles in one pile. However, you may then want to break it down further, such as 'produce' and 'weight loss' and 'supplements'. If you save pictures or reports on new exercise ideas, you may want to separate them all into one pile, first, and then break them further down. Examples could be 'upper body', 'shoulder', 'abdominals', etc.

If you want to organize your files, pick just one drawer at a time to focus on. If you have allowed two hours to work on this project and you aren't complete at the end of two hours, just pick up on the day you have again allotted time to work on that project! I decided it was time to re-organize my office a short while ago, so I first chose to clean up an area that had old personal training client files. By breaking it down into small sections, I was able to not only finish a project I dreaded, but actually see results as I allowed myself small blocks of time to complete it. If you struggle with organization in your office, a great resource is the book, *Organize Your Office... In No Time,* by Monica Ricci.

Now that you have made a clear intention of when you can work on your business, it's time to look at the key aspects of who you will work with, what it is about you that draws those people to you, and how to tell them what you do in a compelling way to make them want to know more. Let's first look at your ideal client.

Review of Chapter 5

✓ Create a master weekly schedule

✓ Opportunity list

✓ Narrowing down the goals and objectives for the business

✓ Prioritizing

✓ Working in the most efficient quadrant

✓ Organizing

Clarifying:

Set . . .

CHAPTER 6

Choosing a Niche

Who is Your Ideal Client?

"I don't know the key to success, but the key to failure is trying to please everybody."

– Bill Cosby

"I can't give you a surefire formula for success, but I can give you a formula for failure; try to please everybody all the time."

– Herbert Bayard Swope
American editor and journalist
First recipient of the Pulitzer Prize

I always hear from new clients that they are afraid to just pick one type of clientele to work with. "Won't that limit my opportunities?" they ask. Actually, just the opposite happens!

If you don't have an ideal client in mind when you write your marketing materials, to whom will you speak to? If you can't visualize that person who you just love to work with, how will your readers hear your passion and excitement? You won't 'get' to anyone if you are speaking to generic 'everyone'; it falls flat and everyone will quickly lose interest. But, if you imagine your ideal client reading your marketing materials (letter, website text, etc), then your passion and excitement will come out in your words.

When you think of Starbucks, what comes to mind? What about McDonalds? What about Nordstrom's? They know who their ideal clients are and they are very specific about the product or service they offer. Hewlett-Packard markets all-in-one machines that print, fax, and scan to segments of the home office market. This is niche marketing and an example of knowing who your ideal client is and narrowing it down.

Why is this important?

Niche marketing can be extremely cost-effective. For instance, imagine you offer a product or service that's just right for a select demographic or ethnic group in your area. One example is that soccer is a HUGE sport in your area. Since you grew up playing the sport, and even played in college under a soccer scholarship, you decide to target teens who want to improve their game so they can also secure a scholarship for college. Narrowing down exactly who your market is can help you just advertise in the media types that your target market takes part in.

Just because you pick a specific, narrow target clientele to work with does NOT mean that if someone outside of that niche calls you that you can't see them! In fact, using the example above, although all your marketing is to teens and their parents, promoting your soccer training, one day a boy's father calls you because his son would just like to improve his fitness level so he can *start* playing soccer. You have actually achieved great success when this happens!

Just recently someone called me for business coaching who was not a health professional. Does this mean I should turn them away? Does it mean they are NOT my ideal client? Not at all! In fact, this person is exactly the type of person I love to work with: They have a passion, a drive and a hunger to create the business of their dreams and they just need guidance, encouragement and motivation. By knowing what qualities in a client you enjoy the most, you will find working with them the most rewarding, and thus you begin to attract those clients, who will likewise feel fulfilled working with you.

Before you can really spend time on your business plan, you must determine what you want to do, where you want to go, and who you want to work with. Address the questions and issues below to help you narrow down your ideal client and discover how to find them.

How this helps increase your success is that you will be marketing TO someone who will hear your words as if they were hitting him/her in the heart, and because you are passionate about that particular 'ideal' client, they will also hear your passion, which will attract them further to find out more.

Who do you most enjoy working with?

Think of all the past clients, customers or patients you have ever seen and allow yourself to imagine. Open the door to your office and let all of those past clients in the door. It may become very crowded, but that's okay for now. Look over all these people in your office, and pick out the one person who represents your ideal client. Take some time to really think about this. Now invite them, in your mind, to sit across from you. If you could not come up with an ideal client then it's okay to create that person in your mind, but still ask them to sit across from you.

What are their qualities, characteristics and attributes? You need to know exactly who you're speaking to. Who are they? You need basic demographic and psychographic information, such as what profession they are in, what size or type of company they work for, where exactly they live and work. How old are they, what sex are they, what do they spend their free time doing? What type of person is he/she; are they externally motivated or internally motivated? Must you take them by the hand or are they able to take your education/information and run with it. How do they dress, how do they act? It's important you know what their values, interests, style is, also.

Look at this person: How did you meet them? How did they hear about you? How did they contact you for your services? What is the expression on their face? What language do they speak? How are they dressed? What makes them such a pleasure for you to do business with them? Perhaps they are always courteous, or always compliant, or send new referrals your way often.

Exercise 6.1

Write down at least ten of these qualities, characteristics and attributes of this person. Take your time. The more specific you can be the better. Here are some examples:

> They respect me and take my advice.
>
> They are internally motivated.
>
> They are consistently cheerful.
>
> They are enthusiastic and positive.
>
> They can afford my services and pay on time.
>
> They are committed to taking charge of their life and health.

Where are they?

> Cindy wanted to target working moms. As a consequence, she found online networks of working moms and started to network and write articles for that niche market.

Knowing where your ideal clients are and how to communicate with them is extremely important. If you target a specific professional group, advertising in the local newspaper may not even reach them and you could spend a lot of wasted money. However, if your target market reads a particular publication, writing articles for that publication will hit right on target.

It's also important to understand the most effective way to communicate with your ideal client. If your clients are all busy professionals who have no time for the Internet, you may never reach them with online networking, electronic newsletters, email and website copy. However, attending business meetings and mixers may be the perfect way to meet them. Just a little bit of research will quickly tell you how best to find and communicate with your ideal clients.

What makes that ideal client tick?

Often the things that are most important in our lives are the things that go unsaid in a conversation. Those are our core values. They are the things that drive us to get up and get moving every day. We may or may not reach our goals but we always live in accordance with our core values. So, if we really want to be effective in our business, we need to recognize the core values of our clients. This will be the key to effective marketing as you grow your practice! This is not EASY! Most of us have no clue what makes our clients click! But, if you want to get them knocking on your door, you have to really determine what those answers are. To help, go back to that person sitting on the other side of your desk from you. Who do you want to see and what do you want to do for them?

Exercise 6.2

Look at your imaginary ideal client and answer these questions about them:

Why do you get out of bed in the morning?

What is most important in your life?

Who is most important in your life?

What do you really love about your life?

What do you most want to accomplish before leaving this world?

What you may start to notice is that you are likely to attract clients who have values similar to yours, so if you can answer these questions for yourself, see if these answers would apply to your ideal client, too.

What your ideal client expects you to deliver

You get to create whatever type of practice that works for you. What you will deliver will be a perfect fit for what your ideal client wants. This is YOUR passion, so instead of trying to fit it into what everyone else wants, which sends you in thousands of different directions, you get to control the path! It's important that you are 100% happy and fulfilled in your business. Then your joy and passion will show in everything you do, which is one of the best marketing tools out there! By getting very clear and specific about what you want to deliver, you will attract exactly the people who will be perfectly happy with what you offer.

Exercise 6.3

A) Make a list of all the services you choose to deliver

(Examples include offering in-home personal training so your client doesn't have to leave his/her house to get fit; supermarket shopping tours; you would love to create a 10-week employee wellness weight loss program; as a sports nutritionist, you would like to work with the trainers in your local health club, starting with presenting a seminar on how nutrition can enhance results for members. If you are reading this book, I suspect you already have a few ideas. Write them down.)

B) For each service you have included above, what criteria do you think will be important to your clients that make that service excellent? Consider such things as 'excellent customer service', 'dependable', 'reliable and accurate information', etc. Consider a service you have received yourself in order to help you determine what would be important to you if you were paying someone for this service.

C) After you complete your list, go through it again. After each item that you have written down on your list, ask the question, "What does that look like?" Get specific. For example, if you wrote, 'excellent customer service', ask yourself exactly what does that look like? Be there!

Time to test

Often I will encourage my clients to find some 'practice' clients to work with. This helps them find out what works, what they like, and what needs improvement. Talking to various people about what you have to offer will also let you know if there really is a market for it! Offering a test newsletter or seminar is another good way to test the market.

Exercise 6.4

Write down ways you can test your market in your e-book or notebook.

Part of testing your market is to go back to finding out what makes them tick. Literally asking them some of the questions listed above can help you learn more about them and understand how best to communicate with them.

Other examples include surveys, evaluations and assessments, both beforehand, or during your work with them and afterwards. You could ask a third party to call and ask the questions so clients don't feel uncomfortable answering the questions and will be perfectly honest. By rewarding people for taking part can sometimes increase the response rate.

Exercise 6.5

A) Write down at least ten questions to ask people who fit into your ideal client profile. A few examples would be as simple as, "what service would you like from someone like me?", "what have you tried (related to your services) that you needed help with?"

B) As a real challenge, then determine **when** you will step out of your comfort zone and ask those questions! Set a date and time in your calendar and go for it!

Just do it!

Now it's time to get out there and do it. With most of my clients, they are chronic researchers and often it takes a lot of challenges to get them out of the planning mode and into the doing mode. You won't know what really works until you do it!

Where do you need to improve?

This final question helps you really determine the services you offer and the ideal client you are looking to attract. This section is for people who already do have at least one client.

Exercise 6.6

Go through the list of what your perfect customer expects you to deliver and ask yourself, "Am I doing this or providing this 100% of the time right now?" This helps you see that you don't have to be all things to all people. You only have to provide the things that you want to provide, and do it consistently. If you answer yes to each of the services, then you are set! If you answered no to any of them, put them on a list of things to improve and use this list to refine what you have to offer and who you want to attract as clients.

Now that you have done all the work above, review what you did for this chapter to review all the services or products you plan to offer (or already do offer) and go through that list, asking the above question of your real or imaginary product or service. You may not have the answer right now, but just going through this exercise will start to make it more real. For more help in this process, read the book, At-

tracting Perfect Customers: The Power of Strategic Synchronicity, by Stacey Hall and Jan Brogniez.

Come back to this process.

This is not the end of the story. Just as with the business plan and the marketing plan, you need to re-visit your ideal client every 6-12 months to make sure that you are still doing what you love to do and that you are still offering what your ideal clients want or need.

> As so many clients do with this section, Rachel really stressed over 'having' to pick just one ideal client. She said that although she really would like to target women, when going through this exercise, all her favorite clients were men! I assured her that she could pick more than one ideal client right now. As she worked further through the process, it would become more clear. Plus, clients can successfully pick more than one ideal client! They will create a marketing message for each client separately. This greatly relieved her and she felt that just this knowledge would help her narrow down who she would most love to work with.

Now that you have determined your ideal client, it's time to look at what makes you special and unique! What is it about you that will attract your ideal clients?

Review of Chapter 6:

✓ How to define your niche market

✓ Determine who your ideal client is

✓ List of services you will provide

✓ How to test your market

✓ Evaluation of your services

CHAPTER 7

The Unique Essence of You

"But find something that you absolutely love doing. And then get to love the way you do it. That's the uniqueness of all of us. That's it."

– Al Lewis

Imagine standing at the top of a huge mountain and shouting to the world what you have to offer, which then attracts all of your ideal clients. In essence, this is what the 'essence' of you is all about.

Telling the world who you are

When you put your first ad or article in the paper, or present talks to a community group, what is it that you are telling them about yourself? Who are you? What will they remember about you? What makes you stand out among your colleagues and peers? For the greatest success in your business, you must be very clear as to what this is.

The clients I see must work through this self-discovery process before they are ready for the business plan. Many people struggle with this step. Until you are very clear about what makes you unique and what attracts your ideal clients to you, and can **say** it, you can't proceed into working on your goals, objectives and services clearly.

Speaking to a room full of people and leaving them with the fact that you are an expert is not enough: An expert in what? It could be nutrition, it could be fitness, and it could be health, but what else?? Again, who are you? Why would they call you? Sure, they may want the information you have to offer, but there has to be something about you that encourages them to actually take the step to contact you.

Below are seven important steps that will help you determine what makes you shine. These are steps to uncover your "Unique Essence"; the foundation of who you are and what you do – your very core, no matter where you are. It's what makes you, you. Once you have done this, then you will be very clear on how to craft your marketing messages to attract your ideal clients.

Step #1   What are 7-10 things that are always true about you?

Exercise 7.1

A) Write down a list of sentences that begin with, "I always..." and list things that are always true for you in your life, no matter what. Look at the positives. A couple examples from me are, "I always laugh a lot", and "I always see the good in people". More examples from others include, "I always make people laugh", "I always hug people", and "I always listen for the deeper meaning". What are the things you are most passionate about?

B) Once you have your list, read them out loud and see how they feel. You'll know the ones that ring true.

Step #2   Who do you specialize in helping?

Exercise 7.2

Write down a list of your specialties.

Specializing is not only hard to determine at first, but scary for a new business owner, as we addressed earlier. You are afraid you will lose business if you don't accept everyone who calls you. However, as mentioned before, if you do everything for everyone, how will you stand out? Specializing actually helps BUILD business! For example, if there was an RD in your area who specialized in eating disorders, everyone would know that they are the person to contact for such issues. If they gave a presentation, people would know what their topic would be on and what services they have to offer. They will become known as the specialist to go to for eating disorder issues. That may lead to requests to come speak to athletes or teenagers, but ultimately what prompted these requests was their specialty. If your specialty is training older adults, that will be what you will focus on in your marketing and promotion and in everything you do. Chances are you will contact local senior centers, as just one example.

As someone who specializes, you can become known as the expert in that field. Perhaps it's working with kids who want to improve their performance for playing soccer, or maybe you enjoy working with people who have diabetes or even people who suffer from osteoporosis. Just because we specialize does not mean we have to turn down others when they call. However, specializing will help you become very clear in your marketing message and will attract your ideal clients, as well as others who see some aspect of themselves in your message to your ideal clients.

Final examples might include working with people with MS, working with kids, pregnant women, athletes, older women who want to lose weight, people with cancer, etc.

Step #3   What are you known for?

Exercise 7.3

Write down at least four characteristics you are known for. For example: What traits would your professional colleagues or clients attribute specifically to you?

I don't want you to just come up with an easy answer, here. Dig into yourself and really determine what it is about you that draws people to you. Ask friends, clients, patients, colleagues, if necessary. When I have asked clients, their answer has been my listening skills. I would have never guessed this if I hadn't asked! There may be an answer in your statement you came up with in step #2.

Consider others you know in your profession. There are experts in celiac disease, experts in balance training. Some people are known for their work with kids, others are specialists who you may think of when the topic of elderly nutrition comes up. I can think of specific dietitians who are diabetes educators, and trainers who love working with women.

Step #4   What are the two or three key emotions your clients experience?

Exercise 7.4

Write the two or three key emotions your clients experience in your e-book or notebook. Now, this is a hard one for most of my clients; they tend to start getting practical. If it is not an emotion, cross it out and try again. It must be an emotion.

If you're not sure, ask **them!**

These are the emotions your clients *want* to experience through their work with you. So, perhaps that is relief, joy, and assurance. What will your client want to feel?

In all marketing messages, this question is of key importance. Until you really define the top emotions your clients want to experience, you will not be able to effectively speak to their needs. Sure, they may want to lose weight, but *why* do they want to lose weight? Put yourself in your clients' shoes. If you already have an office, literally sit in the chair your clients sit in and pretend to be them and ask yourself, as the client, this question. Your client may want someone to tell them their dream really is possible when they were feeling like it wasn't, so they want hope, reassurance, security, and...

Step #5   What main problems do you solve?

Exercise 7.5

Write down the main types of problems you solve. List no less than 5 of each; practical problems and the emotional problems that are tied into that practical problem. Some of these answers may be the same, or similar, to what you came up with in Step #4.

This is where you look at all the practical problems you solve, again from the client's point of view, along with the emotional problems. The practical problems need to be solved, but it is still important that you understand that in order for the client to decide to hire you, you have to know how to speak to their emotional reasons for contacting you. Sure, there are 100 ways to lose weight, and thousands of directions to go to accomplish that, but what can you speak to that will make them feel you are the right fit for them? Again, who are you?

I addressed emotional problems above, such as joy, relief, etc. Some practical problems could include understanding what a starch serving is, or realizing how many calories they need to eat in order to lose or maintain their weight. Another might be moving with less pain, which leads them to enjoy their days more.

Step #6   What is the one thing you do best?

This is the practical aspect of what you do. Maybe it's a particular problem you are adept at working through, maybe it's a special way you have to encourage people to take a certain action. This is something you care enough about that you strive to be the best at. It may even be something that others have told you you're very good at!

Exercise 7.6

List at least three things you do really well.

To give you an example, my answer to this question is, "Help people look within themselves and answer the questions around who they are, what they love to do, what makes them special. I help them create their plans to make it all happen."

Maybe you are good at making people feel special, or have a special technique for explaining an aspect of how to incorporate healthy foods into their diet. Perhaps you are really good working with kids, showing them how exercise and fitness can be fun. Finally, maybe you have such a great sense of humor that the senior population you work with can't get enough of you and the information you provide.

Step #7   Create a statement that represents you in all situations and at all times.

Exercise 7.7

Write down a statement that helps you define yourself. Be sure to cover what you love to do, why you love to do it and how it will be done. Be creative!

Once you have worked through all the steps above, create a statement using those things you came up with. This will be your own personal expression of who you are. This statement is going to help you define what it is you want to do in your business and even life;

who you want to be in the world. Your statement should include what it is you want to do, how you are going to do it, and then include why. Your why is your passion and motivation. It may have some sense of why you are going into business. To give you an example, mine is, "I love to inspire others to be their best so they can create anything they desire. I do this through supportive coaching". I have the three parts in my sentence; one part says what I love to do and why and the other part includes how I do it.

This statement will take some time to create, so don't feel you have to come up with it the first time through. Initially it may be easiest to write some thoughts down, but then walk away from it and come back and say it out loud. Once you have it right, again, you'll know it; it will just feel like you and give you inspiration. You are creating you!

Put it all together

Once you have all the answers from the above seven steps, you then have all the information necessary to create who you are and what you will become known for. This exercise helps you formulate your future mission statement and becomes the basis for your website text. This is you!

The information you formulate from above will help you craft all your future marketing messages. If you have tried to write a business plan in the past, the above steps will definitely help fill in some blanks you may have had. Getting to know your own unique essence will help you make a name for yourself and will also help you craft your marketing message to create a thriving business.

You now have all the main ingredients to put your audio logo together, so let's not delay and get you into the fun part of telling people you come into contact with, what you do so they want to know more!

Review of Chapter 7

✓ Create a list of things that are always true about you

✓ Discover who you specialize in working with and what problems you solve

✓ Uncover the key emotions your clients experience

✓ Create a statement that represents you

CHAPTER 8

Create a Marketing Message to Persuade the World into Action

If you don't tell the world how great you are ...how will they know?

– Margie Geiser

You strike up a conversation with a woman at the supermarket, or you attend a networking event and the businessman asks you what you do. What do you say? How do you convey what you do by addressing the needs of your ideal clients and incorporating your unique essence? This is the purpose of this chapter – to make the person in front of you, and anyone reading your marketing text, feel they have no choice but to contact you for your services! What you say can make the difference between a polite thank you and good-bye, or an appointment as a new client.

Joe didn't realize that he already was very good at presenting his marketing message. The only thing that was missing was his call to action. Once he realized this, and practiced what he could use for a call to action, however, it was amazing how his business started to pick up.

Marketing conversations

Marketing conversations are any communication that generates attention or interest in your services. These conversations include not only what you say during that call of inquiry or when you meet people at events, but can also include conversations with people at supermarkets, airports, during presentations, in a newsletter, your website, or any type of conversation or material you write. In a nutshell, YOU are your marketing message in everything you do and say.

The first contact

When a potential client calls you, or when you meet someone in a networking situation, what is your reply when they ask what you do? For most of you reading this, your answer is you are a registered dietitian or personal trainer... Well, this is the wrong answer! Instead of giving your label or profession, speak to the problem your clients have. This is where you have to know who your ideal client is, which was addressed earlier. Your reply might be something like this:" I help people with diabetes who are afraid to eat anything because they are so confused and worried about their health".

Your target market

In Chapter six, you defined your ideal client. Look at that list, now in order to review whom you most love to work with.

The problem

Every person who may consider your services has a problem, pain or predicament they are dealing with. You need to understand their problems better than you understand your service. You have addressed this in the last chapter to a smaller extent; so use some of what you learned earlier for this exercise.

Exercise 8.1

In your e-book, notice the vertical line down the middle of the page for this exercise. If you do not have the e-book, draw a line down the middle of a piece of paper. On the left side, write down no less than 10 problems, pains or predicaments your potential client will have. You have to speak to how they *feel* because of this problem/pain. So again we are looking at the emotional aspect of the problem. Not that they just want to lose weight or control their blood sugars or look good in tank tops. They want to lose weight because they hate what they see in the mirror, or they want to get control of their blood sugars because they're afraid of dying, or going into kidney failure. Perhaps they have a family member who suffered a similar illness or disease and they are afraid of the same fate.

You are the solution

Once you have addressed the problems your clients have, then you move into the ultimate solution you can provide. Generally, this is the mirror image of the problem. So, using the same example as above, your solution is to take the confusion and fear out of eating for people with diabetes. This is not the 'typical' solution, but the emotional solution. Some people can relate better thinking of this section as your benefits. If they hate to look at themselves in the mirror, your solution is to help them like looking at themselves in the mirror. This has nothing to do with what you do or your process of how you do it.

Using the problems mentioned above, here are some examples of solutions:

Problem – Person wants to lose weight because they hate what they see in the mirror

Solution – Loving what they see in the mirror

Problem – Afraid of dying because of out of control blood sugars

Solution – Feeling they will live a long healthy life in control of diabetes

Problem – Afraid they will suffer the same fate as their family member with the same disease

Solution – Understanding how to live a healthy life with a particular disease.

Exercise 8.2

For every problem you have written on your paper, now address a solution to each individual problem on the right of the line you drew. Include no less than 10 solutions and get to know these well because not everyone will relate to every solution or benefit.

By this time, the person is listening to what you have to say and may ask you how you're able to deliver what you say. Now you know you have their interest!

Story time

The next step is to give proof through short case studies. What was the outcome of one particular client? These are the things potential clients want to know. What can you do for *them*?

You can promise solutions, but potential clients want more than a promise. They want to know if you can deliver your promise. They want to see proof in the form of stories, case studies and testimonials. Some potential clients may want to see client lists, talk to previous clients, get background information on who you are and how you do what you say you can do. Yes, people are going to want to know about you, it's just not the first thing they generally want to know.

Exercise 8.3

Pick some of your favorite success stories; start with the situation before you began working with this person, progress to what you did (no details), then describe the results this client had from working with you.

To further help you, answer these questions:

1. What was the situation before you started working with this client?
2. What you did with the client. This is where you can talk about your process a little bit (keep it short).
3. Results from working with the client.

If you have not worked with actual clients of your own, use a story of a previous person you worked with, perhaps in your job (patient or club member).

About you

If they are still interested, after sharing client stories, give them some background on your story. How you started your business, how you developed your services. If you overcame an obstacle, this creates more interest to your listener. Make this short and interesting; not much longer than a minute, in fact. They won't care about where you went to school or how long it took (unless you had to work 3 jobs to get through school and can use that as an example of how you kept your weight down or your exercise up). They will be interested if you went into nutrition because your mother died of complications from diabetes and you wanted to make sure others didn't suffer the same consequences due to lack of knowledge. They will like to know that you went into fitness because of your struggles with weight, and discovered that you love to teach others to learn how to listen to their bodies.

Exercise 8.4

Write down some background about you that will interest potential clients.

Often I have to encourage clients to allow themselves to use their own story to attract clients. Jerry became a personal trainer because he watched his brother suffer from so many injuries in high school because his high school coach didn't know how to train them properly. Annie's mother survived her cancer much longer than the doctors expected because she chose to radically change her diet. This motivated

Annie to learn more about the role nutrition plays in health, thus she went back to school for her degree in nutrition and ultimately became a dietitian.

Your unique difference

You've seen this before! What sets you apart from anyone else who provides these same services? What sets you apart from other services in the health or fitness field? It can actually be one of the above four parts. Your uniqueness could be how you work with people, or the environment you create, or the type of problem you solve, or even the way you provide your solution.

Exercise 8.5

Write down at least seven ways you are uniquely different.

Examples: Jack has diabetes. He has been able to use this fact to attract his ideal clients and offer diabetes education.

Carol lost over 100 pounds and uses this fact in her marketing message to get the attention of people who feel it's hopeless to try to lose large amounts of weight.

Dani had been suffering from ongoing back and hip problems, mostly due to weight. Because of her lack of fitness and ongoing pain, she became very interested in fitness and health. During her education, she started to incorporate regular fitness into her own life and today uses that in her marketing messages to attract her ideal clients, who are women who struggle with pain and weight issues.

Encourage action

In every single marketing conversation, your goal should be to encourage the listener to take some type of action. If it's a person calling about your services or an audience listening to your presentation, your goal is always to encourage the person to do something. Never let this opportunity pass you by!

If you met someone at a networking event, and you are this far into the conversation, offer to send them an article around something you have been talking about. Then ask if you could call them to get their input into the article and set up a specific time to call them. When you have that follow-up conversation, you can then discuss what you have to offer. If you are speaking to an audience, you may offer a free handout or report if they contact you through your website or if they email you.

Put it all together

You've come up with answers to all the questions above. Now you just have to put it together and make it part of who you are!

Exercise 8.6

Create your audio by filling in the blanks:

"I help _____ (this is your ideal client) who _____ _____ (state the problem or issue).

"The problem these _____ (can just be "people") face are _____ ___ (in more detail, state the problems).

"The solution I offer is (or "when clients work with me, they overcome" _____ _____ (your solution that is the mirror of the problem).

Story of proof is next. One example would be: "I had one client who _____ _____ (state problem) and I was able to help her _____(solution of problem), and today she is _____ (outcome).

"What I do differently/how I am different than others is _____ (your unique difference).

If you are talking to someone who appears interested, determine on the fly what you have that they might be interested in. Offer to send them some information. Get their contact information and set up a time to call them to get their input on what you send them. Or, if they're more interested, set up an appointment then and there, and make sure to get their contact information to follow up to confirm the appointment.

The last step is just the beginning

The above scenario could be just the beginning! From here, the person may be able to see how you can help them with their problem and ask you how they can start working with you. If they're not ready yet, this is fine. You only want your ideal clients, and generally these are clients who *want* to work with you. Just because they're not ready, now, though, is not a reason to believe they will never be a client. I have many people, for both my wellness services and my business services, who initially contact me for information, but don't call me back for a year to start working with me.

There are four criteria in gaining a new client: First, they must trust you; second, they must respect you; third, they must like you; and fourth, they will only hire you when they're ready. This is when the pain is greater than the satisfaction of the way things are right now. If potential clients have not met all four of these criteria, this does not mean they will never be clients. It just means they need to get to know you better, what you have to offer, and who you really are. It is important that you understand that it usually takes multiple exposures to your name and materials before a person is ready to contact you. Marketing experts say it takes seven times to see your name in eleven different formats!

I challenge each of you to put your marketing conversation together and start practicing it. Then, the next time someone asks you what you do and they appear to be your ideal client, you will stir their interest, compel them to ask questions for more details, and prompt them into action, creating a connection that you can eventually cultivate into a potential client. Your business will then progress from one that just pays the bills into one that's thriving and fulfilling of all of your dreams.

You are now ready to step into the business plan in order to outline what you want to create and how you will start to make your dreams real!

Review of Chapter 8:

✓   Learn how to promote your services

✓   Describe the problem, your solution, and who your audience is

✓   Understand how to use your own stories to motivate people to hire you

✓   Develop an audio logo that stimulates interest in who you are speaking to

Getting Down to Business:
Go . . .

CHAPTER 9

The Business Plan

Your Roadmap to Success

"The reason why most people face the future with apprehension instead of anticipation is because they don't have it well designed."

– Jim Rohn
Motivational Speaker

There are plenty of resources to help you create your personalized business plan. Although everyone who wants to build a business should create *some* form of a business plan, the plan can be as detailed or as simple as your needs require. As a consequence, this section is not a detailed outline on how to write a business plan, but will instead highlight some of those details and the importance of its primary aspects. In your e-book and at the end of the chapter, there is a simple, 3-page business plan to get your feet wet, but I encourage everyone reading this to complete a full business plan at least once. Before you even read this section, I suggest you look over that 3-page business plan to start your mind humming.

Although I will explain important parts of a more comprehensive business plan in this chapter, I will only work you through the 3-page plan included in your e-book. At the end of this chapter, you should have a completed 3-page business plan of your own. If you have read the previous chapters, you will find that you've already addressed some of these issues. For more help on writing your full plan, one of the best places to start is at the Small Business Association's (SBA) website at http://www.sba.gov/.

> Allison came to me with the goal of starting up her business from scratch. She had just moved to a new state and was in a position where, if she was going to do it, now was the time. As with many of my clients, she at first didn't know what her business would look like, but then started to see all the opportunities in her community. There were no other sports dietitians in private practice in her area, and no nutritionist there for all the kids in the many sports programs! Just about the time she was ready to start working on the business plan, she decided that the best course of action for her was to see one-on-one clients in an office, which meant she would need some financing. It was then that she started working on a business plan to present to the local lending institutions. Not only did Allison secure her loan, but she also learned much more about her business, and where she wanted it to go, along the way.

This is a hard chapter, I won't fool you. Many people who have read other books and who have taken previous workshops on starting a business start losing interest at this point. I encourage you to stick with it, however. Take each step slowly and spend as much time as necessary to address each section before moving on.

In 1995, after making the decision that I wanted to quit working at the hospital and begin my own business, I started writing my business plan. I really didn't know what I was doing due to the fact that my education was in nutrition, not business. However, I did know that this was the way to start a business – that's what I'd heard. When I came to sections I really didn't understand or that required a large amount of research, I simply glazed over them rather than digging deeper. I was lucky; my business took hold and managed to grow with very little effort. However, not having completed a thorough and detailed business plan limited the business' possibilities because I didn't really give myself the chance to look at the long-term goals or opportunities.

In 2003, I started to investigate coaching as an opportunity to expand my business. In the process of hiring my own coach, I learned the value of not only a business plan, but of marketing. While struggling through my own updated business plan, I made the decision in 2003 to start coaching other health professionals who wanted to start up their own business. Through my own investigation into marketing, I realized that the next step for me was to go back to school for my degree in business.

Once I started back to school and began working with a local SBA program for women, I also wrote my first full business plan and really understood the power such a document can have in discovering why I'm in business and what I ultimately want to create in the future. If I had gone through this process when I first started my business, I would have had better plans in place for the possibility of the growth I had seen, and actually would have a larger company by this time. Hindsight is so enlightening. But, now I can help clients avoid the same pitfalls I fell into.

Why write a business plan?

A well thought-out and organized business plan dramatically increases your odds of succeeding. The business plan contains a description of your business and customers/clients/products, includes marketing research and strategies, analyzes your competition, and includes financial forecasts. It will help you determine if your business has a chance of making a profit, provides an estimate of start-up costs, and helps you discover how much money you need to begin. It also helps you dig deeper into the details so you can anticipate potential problems along the way and potentially resolve them before they occur. We don't consider huge growth as a problem, but even that can cause a company to fail if they have not planned for that eventuality. Finally, if you need to raise money, a business plan will be a requirement. Most banks and investors won't even look at you or your opportunity without a well-written and researched business plan. A well-thought out business plan demonstrates to such investors your commitment to the business and its long-term success, evidenced through the effort and hard work required to create such a thorough plan.

No matter what your goal, look at the purpose of a business plan this way: If a new client calls you and wants you to help them achieve a goal, you have to first acquire a very clear understanding of what his or her goal is! If you don't know what they want, how can you help them? You wouldn't instantly start helping a person to lose weight if that wasn't what they wanted. You wouldn't plan out a client's meal plan before learning what they wanted to accomplish. You can't start designing a weight training program until you know what the client's goals are. It's really no different with creating your business. Where do you want to go and what are your goals and objectives? What is your vision and where do you see yourself and your business one, five and ten years in the future? How long do you plan to run your business and what are your plans for the business once you decide to move on from it (this is known as "harvesting")?

Jackie contacted me after her business had been up and running for one year. She was beside herself! Her business was growing, yet she couldn't manage it, and she also worried that it wasn't growing fast enough. What I learned in our initial conversation was that she had not written a business plan. When I asked her what her goals were, she hadn't really ever thought beyond just working for herself. In the initial questionnaires from her welcome packet, she indicated that she just wanted to make $2,400 per month to help ease the financial burden from her husband. Three months later she had worked through the ideal client exercise, discovered her unique essence, and developed her marketing message. With just those tools alone, her income had exceeded her initial financial goal! When I asked her what she wanted to do now, she said, "Keep growing!" But the next question was how. Without a business plan, she really didn't know.

Mission Statement

Under the General Description of your business plan, you will describe who you are and what you have to offer. However, your mission statement and vision statement are the biggies, the essence of who you are and where you're going. This is why the very first chapter of this book addressed your vision. Dream and dream big! If you dream small, your outcome will be small.

The mission statement is often the lead-in to a company's business plan. It provides the backdrop for everything the company does. The primary purpose of a mission statement is not only to help you cement your purpose, but it is the way you are going to convince your ideal clients to contact you. Your mission statement is the heart and soul of who you are, why you're in business and who you see. It gives you direction and lets your audience know what that direction is. It is a precise statement of purpose. Ultimately, your mission statement will be the basis upon which all of your future business efforts will develop. In a sense, once you've discovered your unique essence, you've sowed the seeds for growing your mission statement.

In order to create a mission statement, you must answer several important questions: What do you have to offer, what do you stand for, and why are you are in business? Although listing it all in one sentence makes these look like simple questions, sometimes it can take quite a while to come up with the 'essence' of who you are in such a brief but profound statement. It is for this reason that it's advisable to complete the majority of the business plan (if not the complete plan in its entirety) before creating this statement.

Exercise 9.1

In your 3-page business plan, or in a notebook, answer the questions:

- Who is your primary target audience?
- Why are you in business?

You may recognize these questions and may be able to use what you learned about yourself in the Unique Essence exercise in chapter 7 to help you. It's also okay if you aren't really quite sure, yet. You can always come back to this later.

Many of my clients ask me about legal business status. Should they incorporate and, if so, what about Limited Liability Corporations or LLC's? Is it necessary to create a business name? What about a logo, etc.? Although you may not have these answers right away, don't let that stop you from starting your business. To help you decide if you should license your business or create a fictitious name statement, check your local government or contact the SBA. In most areas, if you are just using your name and are working by yourself, as a sole proprietor, you do not need a fictitious name statement. You don't need a logo immediately. I created my own logo when I first started my business and didn't actually hire a graphic designer for a 'refined' logo for *ten years*! Again, you don't want these types of details to delay starting your business and earning money.

However, the moment you decide to start a business, do be sure to open a separate bank account so you don't mix business finances with personal. Sure, you may pull from one to give to the other, but at least you will be able to keep track of how your business is doing and prepare for the future. In addition, keeping separate financial accounts and records is vital for tax/financial reporting purposes, as attempting to sort out financial information for the business between two different accounts can prove to be quite difficult and can even appear fraudulent when the government becomes involved with regard to taxes/audits.

To help answer some of your questions about business format, see the e-book. If you are considering incorporating, do your research. It's not too early to find an attorney you can consult with in your state. All states have information on incorporating and details that may help you decide the best choice for your business. Be sure to utilize the services of legal counsel when attempting to formalize the business as a corporation. Many entrepreneurs will agree to the importance of investing money for such counsel when developing the business, especially since hiring an attorney now will likely cost much less than the costs involved with future problems which could have been easily avoided.

When selecting an attorney, be sure to shop around. Just like when selecting a personal doctor or counselor, finding the right fit of personalities is important. In addition, it is highly preferable to select legal counsel who has experience in an area the same or similar to your business. While not a requirement, locating someone with similar industry experience can be highly beneficial, especially considering the fact that your first-hand industry experience, from a legal perspective, may be limited.

Exercise 9.2

Fill out the next section of your 3-page business plan to include;

1. **Name of legal business**. As mentioned above, if you do not have a business name, don't let that stop you; use your name for now.

2. **Legal format of business**. Legal format was addressed above. This can be sole proprietorship, LLC, S-Corp, C-Corp, or partnership.

3. **Location of business.** Where do you want to see clients? Examples include in your own home, in the clients' home, at a coffee shop, in a health club,

in a doctor's office, etc. In many areas, if you are going to see clients in their own home, you do not need a business license. Again, check with your local authorities, however, to make sure.

4. **Business hours**. This is your business. When do you want to see clients? If you will have a building or office, what days and hours will you see clients? If you are a personal trainer, it may be before or after work. If you are a dietitian, it may depend on your clientele. Regardless, you still have a choice. Perhaps for the first six to twelve months you will be seeing your own clients part-time and would like to keep them all to one or two days of the week. Again, it's your choice, so plan accordingly.

5. **Primary products and services**. We will be addressing products and services in chapter 10, when we address the marketing plan. If you are still a bit fuzzy about this, just write down the top ideas you've come up with so far.

If you are not clear about this question, how can you operate and be successful? You will need to detail what types of services, pricing structures, and even how you will compete in your marketplace in a well-thought-out plan. If you strive for financing, this will not even be an option, as mentioned above. When we come to the chapter on the marketing plan, you will start to focus on these details. Needless to say, putting a significant amount of effort into the exact details of your products and services is essential in order for the business to succeed, but for the 3-page plan we are addressing, here, it's just important that you start thinking about those products and services.

As the plan nears completion, one of the unintended but beneficial results of your effort will be to see if you are as energized and excited about the business as when you first began. The odds are if you are able (and even *excited*) about completing a thorough business plan and feel the same or even more excited than when you first began, this may well be the opportunity for you to follow.

Vision Statement

For your vision statement, determine where you want to be in 10 years, as well as your definition of success. Consider financial, professional and personal aspects of your life and your potential business.

Exercise 9.3

In your 3-page business plan or notebook, fill in your 10-year vision and your definition of success. Go back to Chapter 1 if necessary.

Values & Beliefs

Name the following: what values and principles are non-negotiable, within yourself, your practice, as well as with all who you come into contact with (customers, friends, family, et al)? One of my personal values is honesty: I expect that from myself and from others. Another one is promptness: If I say I will be somewhere at a certain time, I am there. I expect the same from my clients. Then ask yourself how these values will be reflected in the way you conduct business. For example, if tardiness is not acceptable to you, how does that play a role in how you run the business and deal with clients?

Exercise 9.4

A)   List your top 7 personal values

B)   Describe how these values will be reflected in how you run your business.

Branding & Imaging

Now go back to what you discovered about yourself in your unique essence project. What are the top adjectives that you would like customers to use to describe you and your business? You can then start to create your logo, company colors, and company tag line. A logo is a design illustration of your business. Often it is the first impression you provide of your business. It's better to determine the name of the company before ever worrying about a logo design. Company colors will represent the feel of your company. To see a sample of company colors, visit http://www.updownleftright.net/list_of_company_colors/. I also suggest you see the examples listed in Appendix B for more ideas about colors. A company tag line is a catchy one or two line phrase associated with a product, campaign or business. The tag line will represent your vision and your unique essence. Again, however, don't let these questions hold you back from working on the creation and start-up of your business!

Exercise 9.5

For your 3-page business plan;

1. List the top 7 adjectives customers will use to describe you

2. Describe/draw your logo. If you do not know, yet, start to write an idea or description that may be forming.

3. What are your company colors?

4. What is your company tag line?

Goals and Business Milestones

We earlier discussed how to set up goals, so now it's time to put them down on your business plan by answering the following questions.

Exercise 9.6

What do you specifically want to accomplish? Answer this question for 1 year, 3 years and 5 years into the future. Be specific, such as, "I will have 'x' number of clients per month by the end of year 1". Aim specifically for achievable milestones; otherwise, how you will know you have achieved that goal? Also be sure to aim for goals which are *realistically achievable*: "I want to make $1 million by year 5" is an end result, *not* a goal for which a strategy or tactic can be directly utilized.

Marketing plan and research

This aspect of your business is so important that a whole chapter will focus entirely on the marketing plan. For a more comprehensive business plan and marketing plan, you may take your plan out much further than one year. In the meantime, however, these next questions will start you thinking about how you will achieve the goals and milestones you listed above.

Exercise 9.7

Fill in the four questions under the marketing plan section of your business plan.

1. What are your one-year marketing plan goals? The question to answer to help you with this is; what will your marketing plan accomplish for you by the end of the year? It's also important that you understand how you will reach your target audience. For instance, you will run 'x' number of ads in the local newspaper your first year, your goal is to generate 'x' number of new clients from that ad. But this is only if your target market reads the local newspaper! Another goal might be that you will present 'x' number of small presentations to local community groups in the year, which you intend to generate 'x' number of new clients. Again, however, be sure that your target market attends these events. Another goal might be to generate new connections for new opportunities. For instance, to point out how knowing your audience and where they 'hang out', consider this: You want to become known in your community for teaching kids how to play tennis and grow your private tennis lesson business, so one marketing technique may be by introducing yourself to the local tennis/PE coaches at the local high school. A specific goal would be to contact 'x' number of coaches by October, to propose a free workshop to the school tennis team members and parents by November, all in order to accomplish the goal to generate at least 5 new clients from these actions by January.

2. List your customer's top three needs and challenges. You worked through this issue in chapter 8 when you created your marketing message.

3. List how your products or services help solve these needs and challenges. Again, you not only want to look at the emotional needs, but also the practical needs and challenges.

4. How are you different than your competitors? How will you use these differences to your benefit? This will be the first time we start to talk about competitive analysis, but a good place to start considering this is to review your unique essence.

Strategies, Tactics, and Techniques

Many clients get stuck here because of the terminology. We've already discussed goals. Strategies and tactics are simply terms used to talk about what you're going to do to accomplish your goals. I again want to assure you that we will dig much deeper into these topics in chapter 10, and that the purpose of this section is to just get your feet wet. I encourage you to come back to some of these sections that perhaps you are unable to really answer. Chapter 10 will clear up any confusion you have at this point in time.

Exercise 9.8

What strategies will you use to achieve your goals?

Strategies are how you plan to accomplish your goals. These are major, and can include, "write a marketing plan" or "research customer needs". You actually use strategies to accomplish goals all the time. Your clients use strategies! It's the 'how'. HOW will they lose weight? One strategy may include not snacking at night. Another might be walking 30 minutes every afternoon.

Exercise 9.9

What tactics and techniques will you use to achieve your goals?

Where the rubber hits the road is in the tactics. This is your 'to-do' list. Give yourself a deadline for each task, so you can keep track of how you're doing. Again, ideally this is for 1 year, 3 years, and 5 years out, but right now just focus on the first year. These are your action plans. Often, people can relate to thinking about tactics when they think of war. War tactics are the steps the generals will take to accomplish the mission. Therefore, be sure to outline specific, measurable goals, accompanied by a detailed plan (or plans) to meet these goals.

To use the example of the weight loss client, one of his tactics might be making sure there are none of his favorite snack foods in the house and when he does get hungry, he has some plans in place, such as drinking water or eating fruit, instead. For the walker, some of his 'to-do' items may include putting a big note on his front door to remind him of his walk as soon as he gets home and putting out his walking shoes so he sees them and can quickly put them on when he gets home.

Budget and Financing

This is another area that health professionals would like to gloss over. I know I sure did! However, just as with your personal finances, if you don't really understand what your needs are and what is possible, how can you plan for the future? This is probably THE most important part of the business plan, the nitty-gritty details about how much is possible to make if you charge 'X' dollars for your services. Will it be enough to make the business worthwhile? Only when you have dug into the finances and created projections are you able to see if your idea will generate an income and, to take it further, help you create wealth!

This section on finances is not intended to be a full exercise on how to come up with the answers. That would take a separate book! If this is an area you are not expert in, finding a financial advisor is highly recommended to help you grow your business successfully.

This section *will* help you start thinking about the important parts of your financial health for the business, however.

What are your expenses? If you have been in business for at least one year already, look back at last year's expenses to help give you an idea. Then, consider the amount of business you experienced from these expenses. Look at the upcoming year, then three years from now, then five years from now, utilize the costs you experienced during your first year to estimate costs for the upcoming years, and be sure to take into account increasing/decreasing costs (such as inflation, marketing, and so forth). If you haven't been in business for a year, ask others in similar situations, search the Internet, or hazard an educated guess. You can always adjust your original estimates as you go along.

Exercise 9.10

In your e-book or in a notebook, write down all your monthly expenses. Use your current check register if necessary.

When considering your business, what possible future expenses may you have? Examples might include banking fees for a separate checking account, any professional dues, website expenses, including the fees for domain name reservation and hosting fees, not to mention if you decide to use a webmaster for your design and upkeep. Software, such as for nutrition analysis, fitness planning, or even financial planning, such as Quickbooks should also be included.

Exercise 9.11

Determine your annual expenses and list in the 3-page plan. Consider all the expenses listed above and add them up for a year.

Ask yourself how much money you need per month, then how much you *want* per month. If you want more than you need or currently have, it's time to go back to your budget and determine how you can best increase income and thus net profits.

Exercise 9.12

What will your projected income be? Consider all of your services, how many clients you want for each milestone period, and add it up. This is where spreadsheet software comes in really handy, but if necessary, just list each service, program or product, what you will charge for each, and how much or how many you plan to sell per month, then extrapolate that for the year.

Exercise 9.13

How will you cover your expenses?

Do you have a savings account, will you borrow, use credit cards, take out a small loan from a bank, utilize funds from an 'angel' investor, borrow from FFF ("friends, family and fools"), or take out a loan from the SBA? Where will it come from if it's not from income? Preferably, your business will support itself, but this is not always possible, especially in the beginning. However, work hard to 'bootstrap' your business as you progress, utilizing creativity and innovation rather than relying solely on monetary funds to grow the business.

The benefits of bootstrapping are many-fold, as you are forced to grow on a 'journey' with your business, becoming more closely attached and uniquely creative as you develop. I have addressed bootstrapping in chapter 2. Allow for life's 'extras,' also. If you have no experience from which to determine what business 'extras' may come up, use your personal 'extras' as your example.

Exercise 9.14

List how you will cover your expenses while growing your business.

The final section is one that actually helps you consider the legacy of your business. How will you exit? Sell? Hire employees/contractors and offer a buy-in option? Close down? Pass the business on to your family? Thinking through this process can help you make a difference in your vision.

Exit Plan

As you review your big vision for your business and your life, how you will exit your business plays a role in that vision. Will you sell your business, pass it onto your children, close it down and just disassemble everything? You may be asking me why you even have to think about such a question just as you're building UP the business! However, having an idea of how you would like to end the business when you no longer want to run it, yourself, will help you through business decisions in the future.

For instance, if you feel that you would like to build up a staff of professionals to see clients, and that in ten years from now you would like to just see a few clients, yourself, from time to time, and then gradually be less involved in the company, what does that mean for the company? Will you sell it to one of your professionals? Will these professionals be employees or contractors? Will your company take the form of a corporation where you can vest a particular professional to gradually take over the company? You may not know what type of business structure you want today, but having an idea of how you would like to exit the company might help you make these decisions along the way. This does not mean you have to decide which type of corporation you would like to form. As I mentioned earlier, you can start your company now as a sole proprietor. However, as you review your company goals each year, and your vision for the future grows, having an idea of how you would like to exit can play a role in the decisions you make at the time of deciding a corporate structure.

Exercise 9.15

When would you like to exit the company? This may be in a particular year, an age, or length of time your business is up and running. It may also be when you have maintained a certain revenue stream for a certain amount of time.

How will you exit the company?

As health professionals, we are very good at helping our clients plan, and we are excellent at creating meal plans for others. As fitness professionals, we can help our clients create incredibly toned or trained bodies by designing effective exercise plans to help them achieve their goals. However, if we fail to plan for our own future, then we fall into the following trap: 'Failing to plan is a plan for failure'. We use tools to help our clients, so doesn't it just make sense to use tools to help our business? If you don't feel comfortable making such detailed plans on your own, don't be afraid to seek outside help from experienced individuals. Remember, your clients have done the exact same thing when looking to you for health and fitness assistance, and there is certainly no shame in that!

Now it's time to go back into the worksheet and review your 3-page business plan. If there are sections you were unclear about or unsure of when you began, see if you are clearer now. If not, don't fret; it's not uncommon to have to spend time soul-searching the answers to big questions about what your business is about and what you will stand for. We will be coming back to the marketing plan in chapter 10. Again, I want to emphasize that this should just be the START of creating your full plan, but at least it will help move you forward. Don't be intimidated, but answer each question to the best of your abilities. Remember the more details you give, the better defined your business becomes.

Without market research and budgeting, your business may fall flat. Many health and fitness professionals shudder just from hearing the *word* 'marketing'. I know I did years ago! My first coach used to say, 'Oh, I just love marketing!' and in my mind I'd be thinking, "I can't imagine ever feeling like that!' Well, a funny thing happened along the way to digging deeper into my business and my own ideal clients: I now LOVE marketing! But even more, I love teaching others how to come to terms with, understand, and yes, even love it!

Now that you have tackled the really challenging job of creating your business plan, let's next journey into the 'meat and potatoes' of the planning, into the marketing plan, where we'll make it all real!

Review of Chapter 9

✓   Determine your mission and vision statement

✓   Discover more details about what your business will look like

✓   Identify your values and beliefs

✓   Start to create your brand and image

✓   Start identifying strategies and actions to grow your business

✓   Determine budget and financing options

Three-Page Business Plan

Mission Statement:

Who is your primary target audience?

Why you are in business:

Name of business:

Legal format of business:

Location of business:

Business hours:

Primary products and services:

Vision Statement:

"In 10 years, my business will be..."

"My definition of success is..."

Values and Beliefs:

My top 7 personal values:

    1.

    2.

    3.

    4.

    5.

    6.

    7.

How are these values reflected in the way I run my business?

Branding and Imaging:

The top 7 adjectives I would like customers to use to describe my business and me:

    1.

    2.

    3.

    4.

    5.

    6.

    7.

My logo looks like this:

My company's colors are:

My company's tag line is:

Goals, Business Milestones:

In 1 year, I will have accomplished these business goals:

In 3 years, I will have accomplished these business goals:

In 5 years, I will have accomplished these business goals:

Marketing Plan:

My one-year marketing plan goals are:

My customer's top three needs and challenges are:

    1.

    2.

    3.

My products/services help solve these needs and challenges by:

    1.

2.

3.

4.

5.

6.

I'm different than my competitors because:

Strategies:

I will use the following strategies to achieve my goals:

1.

2.

3.

Actions:

I will use the following tactics and techniques to achieve my goals:

1.

2.

3.

4.

5.

Budget and financing:

My annual expenses are:

My projected income is:

I will cover my expenses by:

Exit plan:

My plan for exiting the company is:

When:

How:

CHAPTER 10

Creating your Future with a Marketing Plan

Good plans shape good decisions.
That's why good planning helps to make elusive dreams come true.

– Lester R. Bittel
The Nine Master Keys of Management

When I first started to seriously look into writing my own marketing plan, it was with my first coach who separated the marketing plan from the business plan. In my mind, separating things into 'sections' made perfect sense to me! Granted, I did not say 'fun'; it just made sense. And it forced me to actually work on it as a separate entity that I could concentrate on. Without the plan of how you are going to market your business, the business plan is just an empty jumble of words speaking of dreams and desires. The marketing plan creates a strategy for how to make those dreams come true. Your marketing plan is your game plan for how you will run your business, how you will strengthen your competitive position in your industry or location, how you will best satisfy your customers or clients, and how you will achieve your performance targets you set up.

In creating your strategy, you will answer three big questions:

- Where are you now?
- Where do you want to go?
- How will you get there?

Historically in health care, the traditional marketing strategy was, "build it and they will come". And this used to work, too! As a consequence, when I was in school for my nutrition degree, we had no classes on marketing at all! Talking to students and interns, that seems to be changing, but business and marketing is still a small aspect of training and education for most healthcare education programs.

In today's global society, educated healthcare professionals are now competing with others who are savvy in marketing and spreading the message to the consumer to attract them to buy their services or products, leaving those more qualified wondering where all the people are!

Marketing is the management of the relationship between the organization (you) and the markets served (your clients). This relationship is critical to your success, so it's no longer enough to just 'build it'. You have to know how to get your message out there AND create a plan and a budget to make it happen.

Most plans have at least seven or eight steps. These steps include preparing a mission statement, describing the services provided, identifying and understanding the competition, spelling out the marketing objectives and strategies, creating the action plan, and creating a monitoring strategy in order to determine what works and what doesn't. The purpose of this chapter is to help you start working on these sections and answer the questions necessary to move you forward.

If you are working on your business plan with the intention of securing a loan, many of these steps will be included in your business plan. If you filled out your 3-page business plan from the earlier chapter, some of these questions have already been answered.

As you work through this chapter, refer back to the 3-page business plan to help. If you have the e-book, you will find each exercise listed. If you are working with a notebook, just follow the instructions and use the Marketing Plan outline that is described here and shown in Appendix C.

Prepare a mission statement

We've discussed the mission statement thoroughly in the previous chapter. Although there are many, many different theories on what makes a good mission statement, many individuals prefer to search the Internet for examples.

Exercise 10.1

In your e-book or notebook, write down your mission statement that you came up with earlier. If you are still struggling with this, that's okay. Use something from your work in the Unique Essence chapter.

List your target or niche markets.

I cannot emphasize this enough. You have to know who your ideal clients are, and what their issues are in order to speak to them. You have to visually be able to see them in front of you and know what makes them tick. We have already thoroughly addressed your ideal client. If you're still struggling with this, go back to Chapter 6 and work through the process again.

Exercise 10.2

Write down who your target markets are. Again, use what you have learned from previous chapters.

For the sake of this section, I am going to pick an ideal client that we will use for further examples, below. My ideal client will be an adult woman, between the ages of 45-60, who wishes to improve her fitness level and lose weight. Her issues are that she has allowed other circumstances in her life to lead to inactivity and weight gain. Today she feels fat, fatigued, and achy and hates what she sees in the mirror, although she is successful in her career and is internally motivated. She is ready to make changes in her life and is excited to work with someone who can help her.

Describe your services

Imagine everything you want to do, either now or in the future. It's okay if you haven't done it before: If it's a dream to provide in-home cooking demonstrations, include that in your list. You will later determine how to make it happen. Include all details of what you offer, where and for how much. Determine what your prices must be to cover your costs. Don't leave anything out even if you're not sure it's something you want to do this year.

This is not going to be an easy exercise, so don't feel you are the only one who struggles, here. Take your time; you're not in a race. However, I do encourage you to work on this every day. Skip it and proceed on, but continue to come back to this until it starts to take shape.

Exercise 10.3

1. Write down all the services or products you would like to offer, regardless of when or where. Allow yourself to dream and play. You may want to go back to some things you wrote down for earlier exercises, particularly if you were able to come up with some products or services during the business plan production.

2. Now that you have your list, break it down into what you would like to offer in the first six months, in a year from now, and in three years from now.

3.   Now it's time for the details:

   a.   Describe in detail each service you plan to offer.

   b.   How much do you plan to charge for the first service and/or product? For the services/products you will be offering in the first six months, consider what your rate increases will be for one year and three years.

   c.   How will you accept payment? If you plan to take credit cards, it's not too early to start putting that process in play. You may want to find a merchant account. There are many different options with a merchant account. You will want to consider where you will see clients. If you have a lot of in-person clients, you may prefer a machine where you can process their credit or debit cards right then and there. If you do a lot of online work, you may like the Virtual Terminal service that PayPal offers. There are multiple levels of service offered by PayPal that includes one service where buyers of your products and services do NOT have to be PayPal members. Also check out your local bank as well as discount member warehouses, such as Costco.

   I'ts important to ask questions and compare services. For more details, see the e-book.

   d.   Where will you see your clients? Take each service or product and break it down.

   e.   What costs will you incur with these products or services? I know this may be tough to figure out, but spend some time on it guessing as closely as possible. Where can you go for help? Examples are asking other business owners and the Internet, just to name a few resources.

   f.   Are there costs surrounding *where* you see clients or producing products? What are they?

For a detailed example of how to fill this out for each of your services or products, go to Appendix D.

Who is your competition?

In order to know how to position yourself from your competition, you must know who your competition is. Do some research and determine what your competition offers, how they promote, what they charge for services, and what their strengths and weaknesses are. Don't rush through this section. Make phone calls, check the Internet, and ask people you know. Feel free to call the people you find and ask questions. If you don't feel comfortable doing that, ask a family member or friend to do it. This is often a big concern for clients; they either are overwhelmed by HOW to find their competitors, or they are stressed over actually contacting them to learn more. However, it's not a step you can afford to avoid.

Exercise 10.4

Find at least three people or companies who are your closest competition and list them in your e-book or a notebook.

Find out:

- How do they promote their services?
- What different services do they offer and what do they charge for each?

Write down all the sources you used to find the answers to these questions.

This is a good place to talk about how you feel about your competition. If you have really become clear about what makes you unique and who your ideal clients are, the better you know and understand your competition *and can work with them.* This also strengthens your profession because you are able to cross refer clients who would benefit from going elsewhere. Two of my best friends are competitors in my geographical area. If I just looked at the surface, I would only see them as competition to beware of and fear. However, I understand their specialties and passions and ideal clients as well as I understand my own. Consequently, when a girl calls me with an eating disorder and needs help, I can give her Katie's phone number. If someone calls me looking for help with his cycling times and performance, because I no longer work with athletes, I will send him to Ellen. Don't look at your competitors with fear; look at them as venues to help you expand your own business!

SWOT analysis

I would be remiss if I didn't introduce you to a great tool called the SWOT analysis when discussing competitive analysis. When I introduce this tool to my clients, they are first confused, but then love the concept. SWOT stands for, "Strengths, Weaknesses, Opportunities, and Threats". Strengths and weaknesses relate to your company and opportunities and threats relate to the outside environment. This is a tool to help you distinguish yourself from your competitors. Once you have determined who your top three competitors are, use this to determine their strengths and weaknesses, too. It's easy to find a SWOT worksheet online.

Exercise 10.5

In your e-book or in Appendix E is a SWOT analysis for you to walk through. Use the questions below to help you. I would suggest printing up several copies. Do the entire SWOT for your own business and then use the SW (strengths and weaknesses) for each of your competitors. This is an invaluable exercise.

Strengths:

- What advantages does your company have?
- What do you do better than anyone else?
- What unique or lowest-cost resources do you have access to?
- What do people in your market see as your strengths?

Weaknesses:

- What could you improve?
- What should you avoid?
- What are people in your market likely to see as weaknesses?

Opportunities:

- Where are the good opportunities facing you?

- What are the interesting trends you are aware of?

- Useful opportunities can come from such things as:

  - Changes in technology and markets on both a broad and narrow scale

  - Changes in government policy

  - Changes in social patterns, population profiles, lifestyle changes, etc.

  - Local Events

Threats:

- What obstacles do you face?

- What is your competition doing?

- Are the required specifications for your products or services changing?

- Is changing technology threatening your position?

- Do you have bad debt or cash-flow problems?

- Could any of your weaknesses seriously threaten your business?

Carrying out this analysis will often be illuminating – both in terms of pointing out what needs to be done, and in putting problems into perspective.

Marketing objectives

The purpose of setting objectives is to create a yardstick with which to track the performance targets set up in the mission statement of your company. These objectives should be challenging but achievable, so that you have to stretch yourself in order to be innovative, creative, and focused. You can't succeed by just 'going along with the flow'.

Focus on financial objectives and strategic objectives. How much do you want to grow and by when? If you are seeing 10 clients per month right now and you want to grow (which I assume you do), your goal may be to increase by 10% per month for the next six months. You can then calculate this out to very specific client goals.

Example:

Right now you have 10 clients/month that you see for personal training. Five clients see you twice a week, and five see you once a week, for a current monthly income from this service of $3,600/month. In order to grow by 10% each month, you must increase your hours by six per month. This could mean one new 2 times/week client a month, which, when you consider it that way, isn't such a hard objective!

Once you've set up your objectives, you are ready to create strategies for accomplishing them. Get very specific with your objectives, such as how many clients will you have by what date, how much revenue you will bring in by what date, and exactly where these new clients will come from. Who will you market to? For financial objectives, you need to be clear about what growth percentage you expect and then how you will achieve that growth.

Examples of marketing objectives:

- Target market objectives (market share, customers, and products)
- Promotional objectives (level of brand awareness, traffic building)
- Sales (client visits, costs per client)
- Channel objectives (where clients come from; MD offices, etc.)
- Market research objectives (what is objective in researching)
- R&D objectives (product development)

- Other objectives (partnership, etc.)

Examples of financial objectives:

- Clients – Volume and growth percentage (how many and what growth)

- By segments (group classes personal training clients, DM clients, etc.)

- Channel sites – Volume and growth percentage

- By channel (specifically where from)

Exercise 10.6

Now it's your turn: In your e-book, or in a notebook, write down several marketing objectives and financial objectives. Use the example in Appendix F to help, if necessary.

Marketing strategy

Working with clients, I see this as the most difficult part of the process. Yes, people find it hard to really pinpoint who they are and what they have to offer, and they spend time struggling with narrowing down objectives, but quite often they get bogged down in determining **how** they want to achieve those objectives. It's like a block wall, but once they have successfully chipped a hole in the wall, it quickly falls away. Often, if you have made the right choices about what you really want to do, this step starts to develop quickly and easily. It goes from being the hardest to the most inspiring step. After all, this is the essence of how you will run your business. This is the 'how' of how you will make it all happen; the action steps. Your strategies will support how you will grow your business, how you will satisfy customers/clients, how to capitalize on new ideas or services, and how to respond to changing industry and market conditions, just to name a few. This is where the 'entrepreneur' in you will come into play.

Jack and Sally had started their business several years before working with me. However, they hadn't really pushed beyond the 'safety' of consulting contracts. Jack was still working full time as a dietitian and Sally was running the consulting business, which had been doing well enough to bring on an employee. They had bigger goals, however, which were not limited to consulting contracts. Through the course of several months, they diligently worked through all the steps you have previously read about, and along the way were implementing various marketing strategies to start generating interest in their real goal of increasing demand for public speaking and growing their online business.

When we got to the marketing plan section of our work, however, Sally voiced her concern; she was worried they wouldn't be able to figure this all out! That's when I was able to point out examples of what she was already doing that were 'strategies'. Examples of what Sally and Jack were doing were; they created a website, they created and were posting to a blog, they were submitting articles to the local newspaper and to online article submission websites. Jack had set up several public speaking events and had a plan for how to include a call to action during his presentations, generating interest in their business. I could go on, but my point is they were already doing many of these strategies and didn't even realize it!

Implementing your strategies involves making sure there is a good fit between what you want to accomplish and how you're going to make it happen, AND making sure to do this with excellence, and in a timely manner. It's important to be sure that ample resources are allocated to the activities outlined in the plan, and there are adequate rewards and testing procedures to keep track of how you're doing. How will you know when a strategy has been successful? If it is, what do you plan to do, then?

Examples of basic marketing strategies include networking, brochures, ads in newspapers, various programs or presentations, press releases, to just name a few. There is a list of over 100 marketing strategies in Appendix G. Some may cost you a great deal, but there are many marketing strategies that cost you very little or just your time. Gauge what your time is worth and how busy you are to determine how many of these strategies you will do on your own.

Exercise 10.7

Right now, write down some strategies you would like to use right away.

Continuing with my example, I will create some strategies that I'll use to market my services. I have chosen to include networking, writing articles – for both the local newspaper and in national magazines, advertising, speaking and education, just to list a few. I will highlight just one strategy for an example; write articles. The purpose is to become known in my local community, and throughout the country, as the expert on helping women professionals who wish to lose weight and improve their fitness through supportive and educated counseling and coaching.

When a strategy works, repeat it. If it fails and you did it right, drop it. Developing strategies that work for your particular situation and personality will take time and practice.

Create the action plan

Once the objectives and strategies have been developed, put together an action plan describing the steps that need to be taken in detail. This is your actual game plan for how you will accomplish all that you have written about in your business plan. It will include what the specific objective is, exactly what and when the steps will be taken, what results you expect to see, the marketing tactics you will employ and so on. This will be your template for your marketing calendar that you will create in the next chapter. For an example of putting it all together into an action plan, go to Appendix H.

Exercise 10.8

Write out your full action plan. A full marketing plan could be many pages because you want to detail all the action steps necessary to implement each individual strategy.

Monitor results

By monitoring results, you can determine which of your strategies are working and which are not. This will help you identify strategies that generate increased business. Track and evaluate clients' responses to each marketing strategy. Conduct regular surveys to find out what clients like and don't like. Pay attention to website visits and what generates traffic. You can often tell what promotional campaign generates traffic by tracking changes to the number of visits to your website. Depending on your website host features, you may or may not have access to website statistics to track your website visitors. If you do not have stat features with your website, you can sign up for Google Analytics at http://www.google.com/analytics/. It's free and comprehensive. You must attach code to each page of your website. If you have a Webmaster, he/she can do it. If you are doing it, yourself, follow the directions on the Google Analytics site to copy and paste the script into each page.

Client comments are invaluable for creating or enhancing your market literature. With permission, these comments can be used as testimonials. You could create a system to ask all clients, past or present, to provide you with a testimonial. For an example, see Appendix I.

Creating a marketing plan is not something enough people take the time to work on. I have found this to be the hardest part for anyone in small business and have had to spend many hours, myself, struggling over some of these answers. I can't emphasize how important it is to do this work, however. Skipping this step can mean the difference between success and failure. Many people who start a small business are aware of creating a business plan, and stop at the stage of the small market plan topics. However, this document is the template for creating your marketing calendar that will set your projects in motion for the year. You are creating your future with the marketing plan, and then watching that future become reality with your marketing calendar.

Let's take that final step!

Review of Chapter 10

✓ Understand the importance of a marketing plan

✓ Walk through the steps of creating your marketing plan

✓ Determine your services in detail

✓ Understand a SWOT analysis

✓ Create strategies to draw up your action plans to achieve your business objectives

CHAPTER 11

The Marketing Calendar

Your Plan in Action

Action to be effective must be directed to clearly conceived ends.

– Jawaharlal Nehru
Political Leader, India

Imagine the peace you'll have knowing that, through the long process of discovering who you are, who you love to work with, how you will tell the world about yourself, and then slaving through the process of building your plan for the future, you are finally ready to just put it down on your calendar in some organized timeframe! This is what the marketing calendar is all about: The final and most rewarding step.

But this isn't the end! It's just the beginning, because your marketing plan will be an ever-evolving process. What doesn't work will be discarded for new ideas on how to promote and grow your business. Great and inspiring aspirations that you have today will make way for even greater and more inspiring ambitions tomorrow. As you prove to yourself that anything IS possible, the stars of possibility will shine even greater!

But, let's not get too full of ourselves quite yet. Now it's time to put it all down on that calendar and there are several different theories about the value of a marketing calendar. So, let's first look at the different reasons to put a marketing calendar together.

The value of a marketing calendar

There are several ways a calendar helps you: It organizes, categorizes and prioritizes your marketing activities, and it can also help you when you step back and look at the BIG picture by actually looking at a *calendar*. It assists you to get all the things done each month that will help you promote and grow your business, and finally, it can help you evaluate the success of each marketing activity.

You could even create some type of "success scale" for each activity you do. Be sure to list what the expected outcome is for each activity. For instance, you run a promotion for the New Year and expect to get 10 new training clients from the marketing activities that you ran, by the end of February. Your activities, for example include: Placed an ad in the local paper, starting in September; gave a presentation on how to get into shape for the new year, in January; and ran online specials to generate interest in your services, starting in November.

When February has come and gone, rate each activity for its effectiveness. Always be sure to ask every potential client who contacts you how they heard about you, so you can keep track. You did get your projected 10 new clients! When you asked each person how they heard about you, you learned that 6 of them came from your online efforts and 4 came from your ad in the paper. But no one called as a result of your presentation.

If you were to rate these activities on a scale of 1 to 10, you would put ads as a 6, your accumulated online efforts (spell out which ones if you're able) rated a 4 and your presentation rated a 0. This will help you know what worked and what didn't work. You want to change or eliminate what didn't work and put greater efforts into the activities that did work.

Looking at a yearlong calendar can help you plan for the entire year. It can also help you avoid planning events/specials/big promotions at a time that would fall flat, such as offering an in-home pantry make-over program during the summer, when all the kids are home from school; you may not get any interest. Here are other ideas:

- For personal trainers, the New Year is huge!

- If you offer a weight loss program for moms, announcing it to coincide with the start of school in the fall could draw lots of interested moms.

- National Nutrition Month is in March, and American Heart Month is in February. Look up other local events you could tie in with your products and services. Does the city have a yearly 5K run, health fairs etc?

- Are there conferences or similar events you could tie into new service releases with?

- When business is traditionally slow (in the summer for nutrition and fitness professionals), use this time to offer great specials just for the summer. It's also a good time to work ON the business and enjoy the down-time, rather than stress.

- What major sporting or other events could you tie services in with? Academy Awards, World Series, major elections?

- Don't forget to plan in advance for holidays, such as Thanksgiving/Christmas/ Hanukkah. But there is also Halloween, Easter and Fourth of July, just to name a few!

Exercise 11.1

To help you get the 'big picture', print up a year-at-a-glance calendar. You can find one online by doing a search. One company who offers a free calendar is Google

Calendar. Write everything down on the calendar so you can get a sense of what you could offer and when. Perhaps you'll think of something new to actually add to your marketing plan, too! A visual such as this will also help you see how much in advance you need to start planning. The actual day-to-day and month-to-month planning will go into what the rest of this chapter is all about.

Spreadsheet calendar

A marketing calendar doesn't have to be fancy. And you do not have to put your calendar together in the ways I will describe, either. So, once you have a sense of what the purpose of the calendar is and read some suggestions, do what works best for you. The key is that you have all your marketing action steps written down where you can simply look at it and then relax. I explain the marketing calendar to potential clients as the document that will help you sleep at night because the phone call to X is listed and the project that needs to start next week is included. No more waking up in the middle of the night because you worry you'll forget to send a letter out tomorrow if you don't get up *right now*, and write it down, as a reminder!

I suppose we shouldn't literally call these calendars, because they are not in 'calendar' format. But, again, if that works better for you, feel free to put it in any format you wish!

One type of calendar is a spreadsheet that would give more detail as to what you will do each month than just the year-at-a-glance provides you. Across the top of your spreadsheet (x-axis) create column headings representing months of the year. Down the side (y-axis), or the first left-hand column is each initial marketing activity, initiative or event that you'll use through the year. See the example in Appendix J.

From your marketing plan, you already know what action steps you want to take to accomplish such goals as increase clients by 10% by March. It is important to point out that the 10% goal is the result for which that action step was designed. And in that plan, if we take the example from the previous chapter on the marketing plan, one of our strategies was to write a weekly column for the local newspaper. So, in the spreadsheet calendar in Appendix J, you will see "Article writing" on the y-axis. You can include as much or as little detail as you would like. For the sake of the example, I have included more detail than I may in reality. I otherwise may just put "newspaper articles" in the y-axis and then check off each month, with an "X" under the particular month, when I have submitted the determined articles. If you decided that you would present a workshop in October, one of your items on the left would be 'workshop', with indented details below it, as shown in the example. Because you have the details outlined in your marketing plan, you then could start planning milestones to complete for that final product by priority, such as by June you would create the learning objectives, etc. For another example of this type of calendar, go to Duct Tape Marketing at http://www.ducttapemarketing.com/Calendar.pdf, but do realize you can create any type of spreadsheet calendar that works for you.

Exercise 11.2

If you would find this type of blank spreadsheet calendar helpful, create one, now. If you have the e-book, there is a spreadsheet calendar available. If you do not have the e-book, consider downloading the example from Duct Tape Marketing.

Monthly calendar

You can consider this final calendar a good next step to the above suggestion, or, as I have done in the past, myself, use this next one as a stand-alone calendar after looking at your year-at-a-glance calendar to see the big picture. When you look at what you want to accomplish for the year, you need to then narrow it down into specific steps that may not fit into the above example. However, you could also break a spreadsheet into individual weeks as is done on the Duct Tape Marketing example.

The monthly calendar is for a month's period at a time. It is actually a form with columns and rows. It is to help you break down activities by either marketing strategy or by marketing event, whichever works better for you. In my next example, shown in Appendix K, I have broken down the categories into marketing strategies, such as 'article writing', 'networking', 'programs' and 'direct marketing'. These are just a few of the strategies actually included in a full marketing calendar. Use what you came up with in your marketing plan to determine your strategies.

I always have clients first create a 'general' calendar that will include strategies that they will use every month, regardless of the month. The example shown is for the first real month, after a general marketing calendar. If you have the e-book, you will have a full-sized copy that you can print and re-use as both your general calendar and all future monthly calendars. As you can see, the categories for each strategy will include 'comments/description', 'costs', 'date', either of event or by when to implement, and finally 'results'. If you would rather track your activities by 'marketing event', that will work, too. To see an example of this type of calendar, look at the example provided by the Brooklyn Public Library's small business site at

http://somedaysoon.brooklynpubliclibrary.org/s4/si_tool_calendar.htm.

Once you have your general calendar put together, you are ready to create the calendar for the upcoming month. When I create my own calendars, I literally print up multiple pages and hand-write my projects and strategies on the calendar. Below is an example of what I had in my calendar from January 2005, focusing on different strategies than used previously:

Marketing strategy: Networking

- Email to one ____ listserv (which would be one to help you promote your business)
  - ~ Daily (under 'date')
  - ~ Results is a check-mark for each day and four private emails for more information or thanks
- Check and post to ___ community (a target market – considering my target market mentioned earlier, it would be a community that older, professional women may frequent)
  - ~ 3 days per week ('date')
  - ~ Results is a check-mark for each day and one person contacting me for information about my wellness services
- Check and post to (a different) listserv
  - ~ 3 times a week ('date')
  - ~ Results is a check-mark for each day
- Research wellness network on _____
  - ~ By 1/30 (under 'date')
  - ~ Results, "done" is written and that I joined the network

I continue this process with each strategy, which included 'education', 'customer service', 'programs', etc. This is your 'to do' list, so be sure that every project you plan and every program you wish to create for your business is listed! Even reading would be included, perhaps under 'education'. Many of my clients stress over not spending enough time catching up on their reading, so if you have included it as an activity, it is more likely to happen than not.

If you plan to promote your services to physicians, be sure you've put your plan together and all the necessary steps are listed in your calendar. You may plan to collect names and then either call or visit or send letters of introduction. You will already have determined this in your marketing plan. You now are just putting that plan down on a schedule that you can follow and help keep yourself on track.

To help put it all together after the earlier chapter on creating your marketing plan, let's take one of the objectives discussed earlier and put the calendar into play. The marketing and financial objective listed was, "In the first six months, I plan to gain no less than 1 new one-on-one client every 2 weeks, which means two new clients a month. This means I will have seen at least 12 new clients by month six, which will result in a 25% share of the market in my area and generate a total of $1500 from this service."

We only listed one strategy in the previous chapter, which was to write articles. For the details, go back to Chapter 10 as well as Appendix H and review the section under **Create the action plan**.

First, assuming it is currently January, we could look at the year-at-a-glance calendar and indicate our goals under June and December. Some people benefit from that visual of seeing how much time they have to work towards the goal. You could then pull out your spreadsheet calendar and create as a main category, as in our example of the spreadsheet, "Article Writing", and then create indented categories, such as "contact editor of paper," "read paper regularly," "write articles," and "submit articles" to help keep track.

Your final step will be to include these strategies in your monthly calendar. If you come up with other things to do that you hadn't earlier thought of while putting your action plan together, you can always add them! But, assuming you are now working on the January calendar, the plan to pitch an article idea to the newspaper could be under 'writing articles' as a strategy category you would likely want to create, based on your marketing plan.

Again, for an example of a monthly column-format marketing calendar that includes some of the example of "Article Writing", as well as other examples, see Appendix K.

Exercise 11.3

Fill out your general marketing calendar, now. If you have the e-book, you will find a copy. If not, you can either create one on your own, or use the template from the Brooklyn Public Library.

Although this chapter went into details of many calendar options, the hard work was done before you made it to this step. The marketing calendar will help ease your mind as you go through the process of enjoying the journey of running your business; seeing customers or clients and learning what marketing strategies work and do not work. Do what works for your business. Plan it quarterly if that's easier for you rather than doing it monthly. Once you establish your marketing plan, keep it up on a regular basis, just like paying your bills. Consistent marketing wins out. Planned consistent marketing with effective implementation wins out even more. If you are just starting your business and following this guideline, you're off to a great start. If you already have an existing business and didn't do anything similar to this when you launched your business, start now.

You now have all the pieces in place to create the business of your dreams. Before going off to enjoy the fruits of your labor, however, there's one last important aspect to keep in mind – Keeping life and business in balance. Turn the page to walk away with some of the most important tips to keep you sane.

Summary of Chapter 11:

✓ Understand the value of a marketing calendar

✓ Determine how the three variations are beneficial to you

✓ Create your general marketing calendar

CHAPTER 12

Balance after the Dream is Real

"He enjoys true leisure who has time to improve his soul's estate"

– Henry David Thoreau

"There is more to life than increasing its speed"

– Mohandas Gandhi

Many of my clients come to me right at the stage where they have just started their business, yet they have not drawn up a clear plan of where they wanted to go, how they would get there, or what it would look like when they did get there. One thing IS clear to them, however, their lives are out of hand: They don't know whether they're coming or going, and they have no time for family, friends, or themselves. They are literally wondering what the heck they are doing!

It's exciting to get a small business up and running. As time goes on, new ventures come forward, and you realize that all your time, energy, thought, and money, are going into creating your dream. What's even more exciting is to see it actually happen! Yes, it's exciting, but *humans do not live by running a business, alone.* We HAVE to have 'play' time: This is time just for ourselves, time to play with the kids, time alone with a significant other. Time for perhaps 'mindless' fun; watching TV, playing ball, taking a walk for relaxation, shopping: Anything but work-related activities.

It's not always easy to do, however. Many of us start our own practice because we want the freedom and flexibility that comes with a private practice. But, even though we go into the project with the idea of increasing our flexibility, if we don't have a plan in place for our private life, we will actually have LESS freedom and flexibility. And, if your business is based out of your home, it's an even bigger challenge! If we ignore this aspect of our lives, our businesses will eventually suffer. As a health or fitness professional, you understand that balance does not just pertain to our food intake and exercise, but also to stress/life management. If you are truly to be in a position to help others, you have to first help yourself. YOU are the example to your clients!

As my practice gets busier, I will occasionally remember one of the top reasons I started it in the first place: So I could take off when I wanted to go play with my family! Today I have to continually remind myself of this and put myself on the schedule; take an afternoon to go shopping or meet a friend for lunch, take the day to go to the lake with my husband or visit with my daughter, schedule a Pilates class just for the fun of it. If I don't actually do the things that help create the memories of life now, when will I? Yes, I will be able to look back with great satisfaction that my business did well and provided me with security to retire, but where will the memories be of my daughter in her young adult years or my mom in her later years? I don't want to look back and wish I had spent more time with the important people in my life. I want to feel as I did with my father; I spent a lot of time with him after he retired. Around that time, I had my business up and running and could spend 'free time' with him, taking hikes in the woods and skiing with him in the winter. These memories will mean more to me through my life than spending that afternoon writing a new article. I had no regrets when he died. The philosopher Friedrich Nietzsche wrote, "A day has a hundred pockets if you know what to put in them". Where can you fill some pockets?

Now, don't feel you are struggling with this alone. I have to often stop myself from working, 'oh, just a few more hours' later into the night. I also have to make a conscious effort from time to time to pick up a book just for entertainment, rather than carry around the next marketing book with me, so that I'm 'productive' every moment when I have to sit and wait for something. I have not been able to take myself out to lunch without a book since working on my undergraduate degree. So, as I write these words, I also do so to continue to keep myself on track. And just about every one of my clients suffers from the same challenge! The plan is great, but if we just write it down and then file it away, as with our marketing plan and marketing calendar, we will not grow as a result of it.

Let's now look at some tips to help you consider balance in your busy and successful life, suggested from the book, *Million Dollar Consulting*, by Alan Weiss:

1. Continue to learn from others. Albert Bandura, father of the social learning theory, showed in his studies that people who would learn from outside sources are more resilient when faced with setbacks than people who only rely on themselves to figure out new skills and information. Learning from the experience and education of others can take you from novice to knowledgeable professional more quickly than trying to learn it yourself. This points to the importance of networking, which although we often consider a way to grow a business, it is also an invaluable way to meet new colleagues and learn from them.

> Because I learn best from conversation and learning from others, I knew that when I was ready to return to school for my graduate degree, I would do best with a live, classroom program, rather than an online school.

2. Eliminate pre-conceived time boundaries. If your son or daughter has a soccer game at 3pm in the afternoon, why not schedule that into your day? And, if your husband would like to go see a show one Friday afternoon, put it in! These may seem like examples of 'playing hooky', but since it's *your* game, you are the one who makes the rules! Why worry that a client will see you in the middle of the day not working? You are your own boss and can work later that night, if you wish to. Or not...

> Melissa was excited that her business was taking off. As we worked together, she created very clear-cut goals that would mark the success she was after. However, she always felt she had to keep working, either on her business or in her business. So, when she discovered she was pregnant, she was both thrilled and petrified at the same time. How would she keep up this pace? She took some time off to help a family member recovering from surgery, but when it was time to get back into the swing of things, she really struggled! What she concluded was she was just working too much and her body was giving her signals that, no matter what her head told her, it was time to schedule in 'downtime'. Just as she set up specific business goals, she now is setting up specific downtime goals. In fact, she enters this time in her scheduler as 'downtime'.

3. Maintain perspective. Now, what you do *can* make a difference in the lives of others, but if you take all of next Tuesday off, all of life and the future of your business and of your clients' health will not be at stake. Keep priorities in perspective. Sure, if you have a deadline you have to meet by Friday, don't take the week off to fly up to San Francisco just because it sounds good!

> Tyler's business was just starting when he came to me. It was an exciting and scary time for him. With every new phone call, he wondered how he could see more clients.

When the phone didn't ring, he would panic that business had stopped. However, he also has two active teenage boys. When summer came, he wasn't sure how he could work on building his business and also spend time with his sons. However, as we worked through the things that were most important to him, he realized that scheduling in family time had to take a higher priority. So although summer was almost over, he decided to stop working at a certain time of the day, to take half days off on Fridays, and take the whole day off on Sundays. His kids are happier and he is more relaxed AND actually more productive! And his business is thriving and he's enjoying the concept of a waiting list for new clients.

4. **Reward yourself regularly.** I know that many small business owners do not do this enough! In the short-term, allow yourself a long weekend or an impulse gift for yourself. If you met a financial goal for your company, allow yourself a 'gift' or bonus. In the long-term, plan when and how you are going to retire so you can enjoy more play and less work in your later years. Don't allow yourself to work until you die, never stopping to smell the roses.

One obvious way to reward yourself is to take regular vacations. Last year we were able to take TWO! I don't need to tell you that you feel great when you're on vacation! Granted, the stress level BEFORE that vacation may be high, but often there is some time that you can really say you feel that 'ahh' feeling, at least once. You know; you're lying in the pool in your vacation home rental, listening to wind in the trees and the waves hitting the shore just below you. And when you get that feeling, you wish it would last even longer. My favorite explanation of the benefit of a vacation is from Dr. Mel Borins, author of the book *Go Away Just for the Health of It*; He says that every trip is a break from the 'treadmill of daily life'.

5. Do what you think you can't. Stretch and explore new interests and passions! Have you always wanted to learn how to play a wind instrument? Have you wondered what Yoga is like? When was the last time you roller skated? Just as when we were in school and were instructed to take courses like music and a language, we continue to need new and different pursuits to keep us well-rounded. Although you may think that training for a marathon is *not* the best move for you as you get your business off the ground, it may be *just* the thing you need!

6. Avoid isolation. We all need someone in our life. If you don't have a life partner, make sure you have a good friend or a close relative you can confide in. We all need someone to share wins, losses, doubts and joys with. Create a support group for yourself.

As a dietitian, I am aware of the many local dietetic groups that exist around the country. Not only do I have a local association that I am able to network with, but I also meet with two colleagues and friends for lunch twice a month. Yes, sometimes it is tempting to cancel those lunches, but as the afternoon ends, we all comment on how refreshing it was to meet with others with whom we have so much in common. They are like mini vacations from which we come away refreshed and renewed for the next two weeks of hustle and bustle.

With the Internet, it's very easy to create a network of professionals who you have much in common with. Yes, you don't want that networking to mindlessly fill up your time, but spending a little bit of time each day or week networking with peers and friends is a good way to stay in touch with others.

7. Stay fit. I totally believe in the power of working our bodies on a regular basis, and I have no doubt you do too! First of all, as a health professional, we represent what we tell others to do. Taking care of our physical conditioning is showing others that we make ourselves a top priority, and it's only to their benefit when we do this. A sound body does lead to a sound mind. It also greatly helps relieve stress! Although I work with health professionals, it is not uncommon for them to also work hard to make their health and fitness a priority. Again, sometimes we need to add those activities to our schedule in order to make them happen.

8. Rejoice in life's possibilities. Sometimes I feel like a broken record giving this advice to clients! Focus on the positive. Imagine all the possibilities that are out there. Limitations really are only in our mind; if something isn't possible one way, there is always a different way to accomplish the ultimate goal. No matter how you do it, energize yourself regularly, through a loving relationship, a special friend, spiritually, in nature, meditating, watching a funny movie. Even with all the perils and risks of self-employment, you are totally in charge of your destiny! If you have made it this far in the book and you have worked through all the exercises, you already can see the power you have in your own life.

Last summer I was able to finally get out into the local trails to hike the Pacific Crest Trail. It was quite a treat! There was one day, while listening to music on my iPod, I realized just how lucky I am. I definitely was rejoicing that day, as I gazed out on the beautiful forest, the healthy trees, and could hear the babbling stream below while enjoying an ideal summer day in the mountains. I even further realized how lucky I was because this is where I live! We don't always appreciate what we have, and I know I've been as guilty as the next guy. So it's important to remember to literally stop and smell the roses along the way.

9. Help others. If you have started your own business, you have a lot to share with others coming behind you! This is one of my greatest joys; sharing how I got to where I am today with colleagues just coming into the field. My vision is empowerment for others, so if I am able to help someone else take that leap into the adventure of small business ownership, I have accomplished a great deal. I have just started accepting dietetic interns, and learning how much they learn from their rotations with me is extremely rewarding. Get involved in your community in some way, or make a contribution of your time to your profession. Pay it forward.

The road through life of the self-employed is one of great challenges, risks, fears, wins, and ultimate satisfaction. For many of us, once we taste that freedom of being our own boss, we can never imagine working for someone else, again. However, we can be our own worst boss. So, when you realize your boss is making you work too hard, and you find yourself smiling less and stressing more, it's time to step back, consider all the tips above, and put that plan together to create, or re-discover, balance to make life worth the risks you took in the beginning.

Appendices

Appendix A: Chapter 5

Schedule Calendar

	Mon.	Tues.	Wed.	Thurs.	Friday	Sat.	Sun.
5am							
6am							
7am							
8am							
9am							
10am							
11am							
12pm							
1pm							
2pm							
3pm							
4pm							
5pm							
6pm							
7pm							
8pm							
9pm							

*If you work prior to 4:00 a.m. or after 9:00 p.m. add to another calendar you create yourself or get from the Internet.

Appendix B: Chapter 9

Psychology of Color

These are colors that are felt to represent the mainstream American culture, and the qualities associated with them.

Red - excitement, strength, sex, passion, speed, danger.

Blue - (listed as the most popular color) trust, reliability, belonging, coolness.

Yellow - warmth, sunshine, cheer, happiness

Orange - playfulness, warmth, vibrant

Green - nature, fresh, cool, growth, abundance

Purple - royal, spirituality, dignity

Pink - soft, sweet, nurture, security

White - pure, virginal, clean, youthful, mild.

Black - sophistication, elegant, seductive, mystery

Gold - prestige, expensive

Silver - prestige, cold, scientific

Appendix C: Chapter 10

Marketing Plan

1. **Prepare a mission statement**

    The mission statement should clearly and succinctly describe the nature of the business, services offered, and markets served in just a few sentences.

2. **List and describe target or niche markets**

    Be very specific in identifying your ideal client. Include age, sex, income, education, occupation, geographic region, lifestyle, attitudes, purchasing characteristics, etc.

3. **Describe your services**

    Inventory the services you currently offer and ID new services you would like to provide. Include all details of what you offer, where and for how much. Determine what your prices must be to cover your costs.

4. **Identify and understand the competition**

    In order to know how to position yourself from your competition, you must know who your competition is. Do some research and determine what your competition offers, how they promote, what they charge for services, and what their strengths and weaknesses are.

5. **Spell out marketing objectives and strategies**

    Marketing objectives will indicate targets to be achieved across several marketing decision areas. Objectives should be clear, measurable, and have a stated time frame for achievement. Objectives included should be marketing objectives and financial objectives.

6. Create an action plan.

Once the objectives and strategies have been developed, put together an action plan describing the steps that need to be taken in detail. It will include what the specific objective is, exactly what and when the steps will be taken, what results you expect to see, the marketing tactics you will employ and so on.

7. Monitor your results carefully.

By monitoring results, you can determine which of your strategies are working and which are not. Identify strategies that generate increased business. This involves tracking and evaluating clients' responses to each marketing strategy. Survey or interview clients for comments about why they find a service important.

Appendix D: Chapter 10

Exercise 10.3 Example

This is a detailed example to go with Exercise 10.3, describing your services.

A detailed example

Going back to our earlier example, here is how I would answer the above questions:

1. all the products and services I would ever want to offer:
    a. one-on-one nutrition counseling
    b. lunchtime workshops
    c. supermarket shopping tours
    d. kitchen and pantry assessments
    e. employee wellness programs
    f. write articles for women's magazines
    g. create a website
    h. write articles for websites
    i. create online/virtual programs for my target market that they can buy
    j. offer teleclasses, record them, and sell them from my website
    k. In-home personal training services
    l. Open up a small, personalized health club, taking on contracted trainers
    m. Speak at national conferences on my area of expertise
    n. Present a wellness program on a cruise ship

    o. Provide wellness coaching via telephone

    p. Offer group wellness coaching programs over the phone and in person

2. first six months

    a. one-on-one nutrition counseling at just a per-visit rate

    b. kitchen and pantry assessments

    c. supermarket shopping tours

    d. create a website

    e. write articles for websites

    f. offer teleclasses, record them, and sell them from my website.

    g. In-home personal training services at just a per-visit rate

3. A year from now

    a. One-on-one nutrition counseling with several packages – Package A, B, and C (NOTE: You would want to give these packages names.)

    b. In-home personal training services with several packages – Package A, B, and C

    c. Lunchtime workshops

    d. Create virtual programs for target market that they can buy

    e. Present a wellness program on a cruise ship

4. Three years from now

    a. Employee wellness programs with 1-2 contractors

    b. Write articles for women's magazines

    c. Open up a small, personalized health club

    d. Hire 2-3 personal trainers as contractors

    e. Speak at national conferences on my area of expertise

    f. Provide wellness services over the phone

    g. Offer group wellness programs over the phone and in person

5. Details

a. One-on-one nutrition counseling

i. Will meet client at her home, office or at a local coffee shop. Each first visit will be 60-90 minutes long and will include an evaluation of her food diary she previously provided me with. We will determine at the first visit when we will meet for the follow up. Follow up visits will be 30 minutes in length and if the client chooses to work with me longer than three months, we will have her re-do a food diary for analysis at that time.

ii. My rates for this service will be $125 for initial visits and $75 for each follow up. I will raise my per-visit rate when I create packages and have an office, which will be in a year. That increase will be 10%. Afterwards, I expect my rates to increase 3-8% per year, as my services and demand changes.

iii. For the first six months, I will see these clients, as mentioned above, in their home, office or a local coffee shop. By year one, however, I will have secured an office that I will share with another health professional and see one-on-one clients in my office.

iv. Costs incurred for this service will be:

Computer and peripherals - $1,000

Analysis program - $600

Paper and other office supplies - $300

Professional dress - $200

Travel expenses - $20/visit

Total = $2,020

v. Costs incurred for where I will see these clients

If I meet client in a coffee shop, I will offer to pay for coffee.

No other costs incurred with this arrangement

Appendix E: Chapter 10

SWOT Analysis

Strengths	Weaknesses
Opportunities	Threats

Appendix F: Chapter 10

Exercise 10.6 Example

For an example of marketing and financial objectives from Exercise 10.6, see below. This example will continue with the example from the chapter, which is specifically for one-on-one consultations. My marketing and financial objectives would be as follows:

1. Marketing and financial objectives:

    a. Target market

        i. In the first six months, I plan to gain no less than 1 new one-on-one client every 2 weeks, which means two new clients a month. This means I will have seen at least 12 new clients by month six, which will result in a 25% share of the market in my area.

        ii. These objectives will generate a total of $1500.

            1. (NOTE: As you progress past the first 6 months, you will project growth percentage and what that income will look like.)

    b. Promotional

        i. I will contact no less than five local community groups and offer my services as a speaker.

        ii. Expenses will include gasoline and food expense.

            1. (NOTE: You will be asked to detail this out.)

        iii. I will visit all local healthcare and fitness facilities to provide them with my business card and other promotional materials

        iv. Expenses will include travel and printing expense

v.   I will offer to present at all of the local health clubs

vi. Expenses will include handout materials, promotional materials and travel expenses

vii. I will approach the editor of the local newspaper with samples of my work and offer to write a weekly column

1. Travel expenses

viii. I will join the local chamber of commerce and at least two other organizations of interest

1. These memberships can vary from $50-350/year

c. Sales

i.   I will see two new clients per month, which will generate $125/visit for the initials. Estimated costs per client in the first six months is $30/visit.

ii. If I have seen 12 new clients in the next six months, the expenses related to this service will be $360.

d. Channels

i.   From newspaper articles and ads – 35%

ii. From physician offices – 5%

iii. From health club referrals – 10%

iv. From previous client referrals – 25%

v.   From website and online articles – 25%

e. Market research

i.   I will conduct customer satisfaction surveys as well as surveys of potential marketing channels

1. Cost could vary from free from an online survey, to the cost of the materials to print up surveys and possible prepaid postage.

f. R&D (research and development)

i.   For one-on-one services, beyond surveys, R&D is probably not necessary

g. Other

    i.   No partnership planned at this time

Keep in mind that this is just one example of what I may include in my list of products and services. I may also want to offer in-home personal training, phone and online coaching, and various products to help my clients achieve their goals from my website.

Appendix G: Chapter 10

Examples of Marketing Strategies

Circle the strategies you would like to implement in your marketing plan. Highlight the ones you use.

1. Business cards
2. Free consultations/phone calls
3. Stationary
4. Website
5. Purchase of products and services via website
6. Logo
7. Teleclasses/telecourses
8. Radio
9. Free offerings
10. Testimonial letters
11. Positive attitude
12. Audio logo
13. Workshops
14. Seminars
15. Contests/ free drawings
16. Great service
17. Strategic alliance partners
18. Daily follow-up

19. Volunteer work

20. Location

21. Phone demeanor

22. Promotional kit

23. Articles

24. Brochure

25. Articles

26. Professional photo

27. Toastmasters

28. Chamber of commerce

29. Trade shows

30. Gift certificates

31. Toll-free phone number

32. Toll-free fax number

33. Separate business line

34. Answering service

35. Accepting credit cards

36. Flyers

37. Postcards

38. Inserts

39. Frequent buyer discounts

40. Remembering client birthdays

41. Regular thank you to current and previous clients

42. Hand-written thank you cards

43. Send articles to clients that would interest them

44. Hold an open house for new office

45. Invite community/business members to open house

46. Follow up with attendees you meet at conferences

47. Vanity license plate with business name

48. Track all ads for results

49. Local 'adopt a road'

50. Panelist at conference

51. Have attorney review all promotional and contracts

52. Oversized or brightly colored envelops for mailings

53. Announce special offers in newsletters

54. Press releases

55. Targeted list from list brokers

56. Voice mail to promote events or website

57. Competitive pricing

58. White papers

59. Presentations

60. Conferences

61. TV commercials

62. Radio interviews

63. Mail newsletter

64. Email newsletter

65. Yellow pages

66. Enthusiasm

67. Classified ads

68. Quick service

69. Mastermind group

70. Donation to a silent auction

71. Rotary club

72. NAWBO

73. Charity fundraiser

74. Teaching adults

75. Serve on association boards

76. Speakers bureau

77. Demonstrations

78. Online discussion group

79. Write a book

80. Give away a chapter of your book

81. Word of mouth

82. Column in newspaper or magazine

83. Link sharing with others

84. Submitting articles to article submission sites

85. Providing education

86. Brand-name awareness

87. Breakfast/lunches/coffee with potential clients

88. Take an editor out to lunch

89. Press kit

90. Prompt return phone calls

91. Members-only site on website

92. BNI or other networking groups

93. Audio tape interview with guest experts

94. Free gifts with purchase

95. Affiliate programs

96. Host your own radio show

97. Pay-per-click advertising

98. Email signature

99. Referral fee/gift

100. Advisory board

101. R&D team

102. Competitive research

103. Free videotapes or DVDs

104. Audio clips on website

105. Audio or website 'tip of the day'

106. Pens with logo

107. T-shirts with logo

108. Bookmarks with logo

109. Happy customers

110. Tag line

Appendix H: Chapter 10

Exercise 10.8 Example

Let's now take our example and put it all together. Using the example from Exercise 10.6:

1. Marketing and financial objectives:

    a. Target market

        i. In the first six months, I plan to gain no less than 1 new one-on-one client every 2 weeks, which means two new clients a month. This means I will have seen at least 12 new clients by month six, which will result in a 25% share of the market in my area.

        ii. These objectives will generate a total of $1500.

Strategies used (we are only listing one, but you would list all of your strategies)

A. Articles

    a. I will contact the editor of my local newspaper, with samples in hand, and offer to write a weekly column.

    b. I will call to set up an appointment with the editor by September.

        i. I will call and if the editor is not in, I will ask when he/she will be in. At that time, I will ask if I need to make an appointment.

        ii. If an appointment is necessary, I will make one.

        iii. I will drive to the paper to meet with the editor at the specified time. I will have samples of my work with me.

    c. I will read the paper to understand the issues readers appear interested in.

        i.   This is a weekly paper and I have been reading it for years, but now I will focus closer on health news.

  d. I will set aside 1 hour a week to write these articles and provide the editor with two per week.

        i.   I will schedule the writing time into my scheduler

            1. Looking at my scheduler, I can work on this project for 20 minutes on Monday, Wednesday and Friday mornings between 9-9:30am.

  e. Articles will be emailed to the editor on Friday afternoons, as requested.

  f. My bio and contact information is included at the bottom of each column.

B. I will submit 1-3 articles to publications that cater to professional women, in order to increase awareness of my services by the end of 2008. For this example, I plan to contact *Professional Woman Magazine.*

  a. I will research topics the readers are interested in, along with the style of the magazine.

  b. I will start subscribing to the magazine 6 months before I plan to contact them.

  c. I will research topics the readers are interested in, along with the style of the magazine.

  d. I will contact Professional Woman Magazine by September to pitch an idea of writing an article.

        i.   I will begin by sending out an email of inquiry.

        ii. I will follow up with the response. If no response, I will call the editor of the magazine.

        iii. My intention, when I contact the editor, is to find out who I should contact with my topic idea and how we can work together.

  e. I will negotiate the pay and then schedule an average of 5 hours a week to write the article and do the necessary research.

    i.   I will research what average pay is for this publication before we discuss this topic.

    f.   I will schedule 1 hour a day, Monday through Friday, between 10-11am for this project.

    g.   I will remain in contact with the editor so that I understand the steps necessary and if or how often they would like to review my project. When the project is complete, I will discuss with the editor the process for submitting it and when to expect payment.

Result expected is greatly increased visibility among professional women who would be interested in my services. Increased traffic to my website will also result, creating a following of potential clients for the future.

Costs involved will be my time as well as the cost of postage, phone calls and purchasing the magazines. This would be;

- Travel - $50
- Phone calls - $25

Appendix I: Chapter 10

How to Ask for a Testimonial

Although health professionals have shied away from testimonials, the public takes them very seriously, and they can make the difference between a client contacting you or someone else.

It is common to include a request for a testimonial along with your request for an evaluation of your services, at the time your services have been completed or terminated. If you are creating a new website or you have clients who will be working with you for a long time, it is also okay to contact them while still working with them. Most clients are happy to comply!

You can ask clients either verbally, by letter, or by email. It all depends on your comfort level, when you ask them, and how comfortable they are with providing you with something in writing, themselves.

Instead of asking them to just write something about working with you, it is best to ask a very specific question, such as, "Describe what you liked most about working with me." Or "State what you accomplished through our work together."

Finally, you want to give clients the choice of how much, or how little, information they feel comfortable to share about themselves. I have had clients who love the opportunity to share their website and contact information but also have had clients who are willing to provide a testimonial, but only feel comfortable with their initials. It's important that you give them that option: You can state or write, "Please provide your full name, title and city. If you have a website, feel free to provide that, also. If you are not comfortable with that much information, just your initials and city are fine.

Appendix J: Chapter 11

Spreadsheet Calendar Example

Instructions: Make copies of this chart. Fill in the month/year along the top – there are enough spaces for 6 months at a time.

Article Submission

Article Writing						
Contact editor of paper						
Read paper regularly						
Write articles						
Submit articles						
Cost Analysis						
Newsletter						
Site Location						
Survey						
Website						
Workshop						
Conduct survey						
Determine location						

Appendix K: Chapter 11

Marketing Calendar

JANUARY

Market Strategy or Marketing event	Cost	Comments	Date	Results
ARTICLE WRITING				
Newspaper				
Contact editor		Propose	By 15th	
Read paper daily	$20/yr	Understand	Fridays	
Write articles		20 minutes qd	M,W,F	
Submit articles			Fridays	
Prof. Woman Mag				
Activities				
Etc.				
Other writing				
Networking				
Specific activity				
Step 1		why	when	
Step 2				
Etc.				
PROGRAMS				
Program 1 project				
Daily to-do				
Weekly to-do				
Monthly to-do				
Program 2 project				
DIRECT MARKETING				
Item 1				
Step 1		Why	when	
Step 2				
Step 3				

Glossary

Angel Investors ("Angels") – Angels are usually individuals who are willing to loan a small startup company larger amounts of money than family members have access to, but smaller amounts of money than a VC would lend. Often an Angel is a successful retired business owner who wishes to lend a new company and also offer counsel and guidance.

Article Submission Sites – Websites authors can send articles to where publications, websites and newsletters go for content. In exchange for running an author's article, the user agrees to include the author's bio and any contact information the author chooses to include. This is a strategy for increasing traffic to a website.

Brand Awareness – Brand awareness is achieved when customers recognize your existence and what you offer.

Demographics – Selected population characteristics, such as race, age, income, education, employment, location, etc. Important aspects when researching a target market.

Fictitious Name Statement – Also known as 'dba' (doing business as). An 'assumed' name a person or people will do business under. The FNS must be filed through the local county clerk's office. FNSs can be Trademark protected.

Harvesting – How a business will end. Options include selling, closing the doors, bankruptcy, passing down to heirs, etc. A company should consider their harvest plans in order to understand what they want to ultimately create.

LLC – Limited Liability Corporation. An LLC combines the best attributes of a corporation and a partnership. An LLC can be taxed as a partnership unless it chooses to be taxed as a corporation.

Market Research – The process of gathering, recording and analyzing data and information about clients, competitors and the market. This often helps create a business plan and can be used to determine who will buy your product or service, based on determined variables.

Market Share – The percentage or proportion of the total available market or market segment serviced by a company. Increasing market share is often an important objective for companies.

Mastermind Group – A group of people who work together to help each other grow with particular individual objectives. Generally a mastermind group will help an person accomplish goals faster than they will by themselves, or help move a person into areas they otherwise hesitate to move into.

Merchant Account – A specialized bank account issued by a merchant processing bank that allows a business to accept credit cards or other forms of payment cards.

Mission Statement – A mission statement defines the reason for existence for the business or person. It embodies goals, ambitions, and philosophies. It is the statement of purpose.

Niche Marketing – Targeting a specific, narrowly defined and focused portion of the market.

Psychographics – Any attributes that relate to personality, values, attitudes, interests, or lifestyles. These are the important aspects to understand about a target market, which explain why they purchase certain products or services.

Quickbooks – An accounting software program.

SBA (Small Business Association) – Independent agency of the government to aid, counsel, assist and protect the interests of small businesses.

SBA Loan – Small Business Association Loan. A business loan from the Small Business Association. An SBA loan is provided by a private-sector lender (such as a bank) and guaranteed by the SBA. Many of these programs are for small businesses that are unable to secure financing through normal lending channels.

Search Engine Optimization ("SEO") – The process of improving the amount of traffic to a website from search engines.

Sole Proprietor – One person doing business by him/herself. A person can be a sole proprietor under his/her own name or under a 'dba'. Taxes are filed under the person's personal income taxes and there is no liability protection, which puts the owner's personal assets at risk.

Strategies – A plan of action designed to achieve a particular goal. A marketing strategy is a process that helps a company decide where they will put their resources in order to achieve the greatest results.

Tactics – Immediate actions created to implement a particular strategy created to achieve an objective.

Tag Line – A one or two line description that often comes after the company logo or name. It's a form of branding as a memorable phrase that will sum up the tone of the company or product. Tag lines can be copyrighted.

Toastmasters International – A non-profit educational organization that teaches public speaking and leadership skills. By joining and attending regular local club meetings, a budding speaker can greatly enhance their speaking skills.

Venture Capitalists ("VCs") – Professional investors who invest in new or developing businesses. VCs usually invest at least $1 to $3 million in companies with a great potential for fast and significant growth. In exchange, VCs expect some control of the company.

Index

About the Author

Marjorie Geiser is a business start-up coach who specializes in helping service professionals create the businesses of their dreams. Her clients come to her full of desire, fear and uncertainty, and by the completion of her program they are not only self-assured and confident, but on their way to building thriving and powerful businesses beyond their imaginations.

Margie started her own business, MEG Fitness, in 1996, providing in-home personal training and nutrition counseling to unfit adults. In 2003, with the business booming, she started to investigate alternative ways to grow the business and discovered life coaching. As a result, she began coaching other fitness and nutrition professionals who wanted to start up a business. In 2005, she returned to school for an MBA in Entrepreneurship, and in 2006, she started MEG Enterprises, Inc, specifically to provide business coaching. As a graduate of the Coach Training Institute, Margie combines her coaching expertise with her business knowledge to create a unique program. She not only helps clients put together the necessary plans to start a business, but also coaches them to dig into themselves to investigate any limiting conversations they have around aspects of business and marketing.

Margie graduated from Loma Linda University in 1990 and is a registered dietitian. She is a student at California State, San Bernardino, studying for her MBA, Entrepreneurship, and plans to graduate in 2009. She is certified through the National Strength & Conditioning Association (NSCA) as a NSCA-CPT. She is currently the Chair of the NE Coaches group of the American Dietetic Association (ADA) and for 5 years was on the executive committee for NSCA's Personal Trainer's Special Interest Group (SIG). She is also part of the ongoing workgroup for the American Council on Exercise (ACE), involved in updating and renewing advanced personal training certificate exams.

Quick Order Form

To contact MEG Enterprises/California Based Publishing:
    Email – justjump@californiabasedpublishing.com
    Phone – 909-867-7317
    Mail – P. O. Box 1207, Running Springs, CA. 92382

For more information, check appropriate line below and fax this form to (866) 480-7082

___ "Just Jump: The No-Fear Business Start-up Guide for Health and Fitness Professionals"

___ "Just Jump" Companion E-Book

___ Upcoming Speaking Engagements/ Workshops

___ Business Start-up Coaching and Consulting

___ "Just Jump" Teleclass programs

To order a book, call or email or go to http://www.californiabasedpublishing.com.
To pay by credit card from this form, fill out the entire form and fax to (866) 480-7082. Notification will be sent when this form is received.

Name: _____Title: _____

Company Name: _____

Mailing Address: _____

Phone number: _____ Fax number: _____

E-mail address: _____

Credit card information: ___ Visa___ MasterCard___ American Express

Please send me ($29.95) x _____ copies of *Just Jump*

Please send me ($34.95) x _____ copies of *Just Jump* with companion e-book

   *Sales tax: Please add 7.75% for all orders shipped to California addresses ($2.32 per book).

Shipping: For orders shipped to US addresses, please add $4.00 for the first book and $2.00 each additional book. For international orders, add $9.00 for the first book and $5.00 each additional book.
        Total book $_____
        Sales tax $_____
        Shipping $_____
        Total $_____

Card number: _____Expiration Date: _____
CSC (back of cc, or front of AE): _____

Name on Card: _____

Credit card address: _____

                     _____

Cardholder's signature: _____

Check here if sending a check _____ (Make check payable to *California Based Publishing*)

I authorize California Based Publishing to charge the above credit card account for merchant services in the amount for products purchased, including appropriate tax and shipping.

Printed in the United States
116994LV00003B/82-174/P